WHAT'S YOUR SCORING AVERAGE ON THESE TWO-POINT QUESTIONS?

- Can you name the only coach in the NBA who wears a goatee?

- Which star set five NBA records last season?

- Can you name the player generally regarded as "the best sixth man in the league"?

- Who was rookie-of-the-year in the NBA in the '65-'66 season?

- Can you name the three players who are also coaches this season?

- About which NBA star is it said, "If you saw him getting dressed you'd have to applaud"?

If your score isn't perfect now, you'll sink 100 per cent of the shots after you've read these and many other fascinating facts in BASKETBALL STARS OF 1967

BERRY STAINBACK, Managing Editor
of **Sport** Magazine, is the author
of **Football Stars of 1966**, published by Pyramid, and two
other books. He lives with his
wife, Rita, and children, Dawn,
age 8, and Deron, age 6, in
Queens, New York.

BASKETBALL
STARS
OF 1967

BERRY STAINBACK

PYRAMID BOOKS • NEW YORK

To my mother and father

BASKETBALL STARS OF 1967

A PYRAMID BOOK
Pyramid edition published November, 1966

PYRAMID BOOKS are published by Pyramid Publications, Inc.
444 Madison Avenue, New York, New York 10022, U.S.A.

TABLE OF CONTENTS

The Season Past

The big story of the 1965–66 National Basketball Season was the Philadelphia 76ers' beating out the Boston Celtics for the Eastern Division title. Boston fooled all the experts by losing the title for the first time in ten years, but they didn't exactly blow it, as Celtic coach Red Auerbach pointed out. The 76ers had to win their last ten games to edge the Celtics by a game.

On the night Philadelphia won the title, the members of the team went fittingly wild. "After ten years—ten years," said 33-year-old Al Bianchi. "We did it ourselves. I've never been happier." He spoke for his teammates, who screamed and yelled deliriously in their locker room in Baltimore. There was a bizarre mishap that could have had tragic consequences. Somebody in pouring champagne over a teammate had yanked a fluorescent fixture from the ceiling and live wires dangled into the wet room. Someone quickly shut off the power to eliminate the danger of electrocution. The 76ers kept right on celebrating in the darkness, and one player yelled, "Turn the lights back on, nothing can hurt us now."

He was wrong, of course. The Celtics were soon to hurt them badly, easily eliminating Philadelphia from the playoffs as all the 76ers but Wilt Chamberlain seemed to lose their touch.

The Celtics, on the other hand, again fooled all the experts. They had a lot of injuries during the season, Bill Russell didn't display his consistently great game of the past all the way, they missed Tommy Heinsohn's fine shooting, and they looked old at times. But Auerbach said, "I'm proud of this team. Sure, we finished second, but this team is the best that ever wound up second in this league. If we went down real bad, I'd feel real bad. But

7

this team lost only 26 (of 80) games. Los Angeles lost 35 and won the Western Division title."

The Celtics started poorly in the playoffs, losing two of their first three games, and were only a game away from being eliminated by the Cincinnati Royals. But the Celtics came back, won two straight from Cincinnati, beat Philadelphia, then beat the Los Angeles Lakers in a seven-game series. It was Boston's eighth successive world championship—an unparalleled achievement—and ninth in the last ten seasons.

The most socially significant story of the NBA year was Red Auerbach's naming Bill Russell to succeed him as coach of the Celtics. Russell became the first Negro in such an overall leadership position in the history of major professional sports and this will no doubt ultimately open doors to other qualified Negroes in the future. Many people, for example, felt Earl Lloyd, the assistant coach for the Pistons under both Charley Wolf and Dave De-Busschere until he accepted a job in industry early last season, was qualified to coach the Detroit team. The Pistons management was not ready to make such a move at the time Wolf was fired, and DeBusschere got the job.

At the press conference at which it was announced that Russell would coach the Celtics this season, Bill said, "I consider this one of the most personal challenges I've had in the past ten years. When Red first asked me if I'd take the job, I thought he was putting me on. Then he assured me he sincerely wanted me. My first consideration was the team. Then I figured that I could do the job and also could stand the aggravation that goes with coaching. I finally decided it might be a lot of fun.

"I'm pleased, proud and happy. Once again the Celtics are making National Basketball Association history—not only on the court but on the bench."

On his retirement, the most successful coach in any pro sport ever, Red Auerbach, said, "They all had their shots at me and the Celtics, and they had time to get us this season. I said I was retiring last January when our team was down and hurting from injuries. But we beat them all. They had that run at us and that is what makes me so satisfied about this championship and my retirement."

Auerbach will coach one more time, though, in the NBA All-Star game in San Francisco on January 10. The league's board of governors named Auerbach to handle the East team for the eleventh time. In last season's game Red's squad overwhelmed the West by a 137-94 score. Adrian Smith of the Royals, the most unlikely man to make the All-Star team, led the scorers on both sides with 24 points and won the game's most-valuable-player award. He received a $5,000 7-Litre Ford convertible for the honor.

A man who also benefited that evening in Cincinnati was Maurice Stokes, the former Royal All-Star who has been hospitalized with encephalitis since the 1956-57 season. Stokes was at courtside in a wheelchair and received a $1,000 check for the Stokes Fund from the Anheuser-Busch Brewing Company.

Maurice made another rare appearance out of the hospital in March when Cincinnati fans honored retiring Royal star Jack Twyman. Twyman, one of the great human beings in all of sports, has worked tirelessly over the years for his friend and former teammate. Jack set up the Stokes Fund after Maurice was stricken with the mysterious illness and has been closer than a brother to Stokes ever since. Stokes himself has battled back from the often-fatal disease and has all of his reasoning powers even though he still cannot talk. But his painfully slow rehabilitation has nevertheless been remarkable.

And on the night some 10,000 fans presented Twyman with gifts that included a new Bonneville convertible and on a night when he scored 39 points in a season in which he had mostly sat on the bench, Jack talked about his friend. "It has been my privilege," Twyman said, "to be exposed to a man with the guts that he has displayed through the years. He has shown Carol (Mrs. Twyman) and me how to live and has given me and my family a fine sense of values." Twyman gave Stokes much and will continue to give . . . and the NBA has lost much with the retirement of Jack Twyman.

The NBA expanded last season to ten teams and voted to add two more teams, bringing the league total to 12, before the 1968-69 season. The new team is the Chicago Bulls, which are owned by Dick Klein. He paid $1,600,000 for two players from each of the nine veteran teams and didn't even get to make a draft selection until after the other teams had gone through the first round. But probably the most intriguing aspect of the NBA expansion was why it had decided to go into Chicago again when the last team there, now known as the Bullets of Baltimore, did so badly.

Perhaps this was due to the fact that the league itself is drawing better every year now. Last season's attendance was up 15 per cent over the '65 total. ABC-TV's national television coverage of the NBA games on Sunday afternoons will continue next year and will be shown in color for the first time. ABC reported its television audience total for NBA games increased by 28 per cent last season.

In college basketball, coach Adolph Rupp's Kentucky Wildcats were voted the national basketball champions by the United Press International Board of Coaches at the end of the regular season. It was the third time Kentucky had won the title (the last being in 1952) and no other college has ever won more than two national championships. The Wildcats, with virtually the same players who won only 15 of 25 games the previous year (the worst record in Rupp's 36 years at Kentucky), were truly a surprise team. They won their first 23 games before being upset by Tennessee.

Another team that wasn't rated in the pre-season polls but which ranked third at season's end was Texas Western, which also had a 23-1 record. The Miners from El Paso, Texas, then beat Utah in the National Collegiate Athletic Association tournament and went into the finals for the first time in history. Kentucky defeated Duke in the semifinals and was favored to beat Texas Western for the championship on the strength of its fine shooting. But the ball-hawking Miners, led by junior Bobby Joe Hill, disrupted the Wildcat offense with their own tenacious defense and won the title, 72–65. Duke beat Utah in the consolation game for third place.

In New York's National Invitational tournament, NYU got into the finals for the first time in 18 years by beating Villanova. But the Violets couldn't match Brigham Young's height under the boards, particularly that of 6-11 Craig Raymond. Stan Watts' fine team simply out-classed NYU, winning 97-84. Villanova defeated Army in the consolation game.

The most disappointing college team last year was probably defending champion UCLA. But coach Johnny

Wooden had three high-school All-Americas on his undefeated freshman squad, including Lew Alcindor. UCLA could very well come back with a national championship team this season.

NATIONAL BASKETBALL ASSOCIATION

Eastern Division

PHILADELPHIA 76ERS: During the last regular season, the 76ers beat out the Boston Celtics by a game, and they should be able to do at least as well again. Whether they can beat the Celtics in a short playoff series is something else; the smart money might well go with the Celtics because of their amazing history of winning the big ones when they had to. But Philadelphia was a physically stronger team than the aging Celtics a year ago, and that fact won't change. Also, the 76ers have strengthened themselves more than the Celtics have. Philadelphia lost two guards to the Bulls, Al Bianchi and Gerry Ward. The latter's great defensive ability will be missed on occasion, but the playmaking ability and all-round skills of No. 1 draft choice Matt Guokas of St. Joseph's should more than compensate for Ward's loss. And Larry Costello, who retired last season reportedly because of dissatisfaction with Dolph Schayes, is returning to the pros now that Alex Hannum is coaching the team. Costello was always a better ballplayer than Bianchi. Hal Greer and Wally Jones round out a solid and deep backcourt foursome. Greer had another of his typically fine seasons in '65–66, averaging 22.7 points per game and leading the team in assists with 384. Jones's shooting picked up considerably in his second pro season, and there never has been any question about his playmaking abilities. The 76er frontcourt is equally strong and well-balanced—Chet Walker, Billy Cunningham, Luke Jackson, and Dave Gambee. Walker had his best season a year ago, averaging 15.3 points per game. Jackson's physical problems affected his shooting, but there was nothing wrong with his rebounding. Look for him to bounce back strong this season. Look for Cunningham to improve quite a bit in his second season as well. As for the center position, the 76ers have the No. 1 man in the league now—Wilt Chamberlain. He put it all together last year, scoring, rebounding, defending, passing. He knows exactly how to play this game to win now . . . and no one in the league wants to win more than Chamberlain.

BOSTON CELTICS: The world champions have lost depth from last year's squad, but that won't be sorely felt. Willie Naulls, once a great-shooting cornerman, couldn't hit much of anything in '65–66 and has retired. Ron Bonham, the former University of Cincinnati star, who showed nothing as a pro guard except a shooting touch, and too little of that, has gone to Chicago. With him went big John Thompson, who didn't get much chance to play. But new coach Bill Russell has all the men back who helped win the championship. He has good balance and experience all around. Defensive star Satch Sanders and Don Nelson will start in the frontcourt, assuming Russell plans to continue to use John Havlicek as a swing man at both forward and guard. (Havlicek had more minutes played than any other Celtic last season except for Russell and K. C. Jones.) The reserve cornerman is seven-foot Mel Counts, who shoots very well but has trouble playing quick men on defense. Another likely reserve is Ron Watts, a burly 6-6 rebounder who must learn to shoot. He was released after one game a year ago but hung around and practiced with the Celtics all season, and Russell likes his rugged board work. But what Boston really needs is a young Willie Naulls—a good-shooting cornerman. The backcourt, in addition to Havlicek, features nine-year-man Sam Jones and K. C., who plans to retire after this season to coach the Brandies team. Larry Siegfried averaged 13.7 points per game at guard playing just over half the time, and he gets better every season. With a new incentive, you can count on Russell's being more consistent if he's physically fit. So the Celtics will again be tough and may even win another NBA championship, but we don't see them winning the regular-season title.

CINCINNATI ROYALS: The Royals finished 15 games ahead of the New York Knickerbockers, and their 45-35 record matched that of the Lakers, who won in the Western Division. Small wonder Cincinnati petitioned the league to return to that conference it was shifted from a few years ago. The Royals would definitely come out better in the final standings. The team simply has no big man to battle Wilt Chamberlain and Bill Russell on anything like equal terms. Wayne Embry works hard but can't do it at 6-8. Now the Royals must also contend with Walt Bellamy in their division. Coach Jack McMahon hopes his No. 1 draft choice, 6-11 Walt Wesley of Kansas, will fill his center deficit. Otherwise, Cincinnati has an excellent first line and lacks only depth. Oscar Robertson is the league's best all-round guard and Jerry Lucas is one of the three top all-round forwards. Wesley has been known mostly for his shooting in college, but that's not what a team with Robertson and Lucas needs. It needs help for Lucas on the boards and defensive play that will hold off the Russells, Chamberlains and Bellamys. Starting with Oscar in the backcourt is Odie Smith, coming off his best season (18.4 points-per-game average). Starting at the corner opposite Lucas is Happy Hairston, who's coming off his best season, too (14.1-points-per-game average). Tom Hawkins and Connie Dierking are only adequate forward reserves. Jon McGlocklin showed pro potential as a rookie guard.

NEW YORK KNICKERBOCKERS: If the Royals continue to have troubles in their pivot position, the Knicks could definitely make a determined run at them for third place in the Eastern Division. This is a coming team, make no mistake about it. New York has its best center ever in Walt Bellamy, and he can be ably spelled by Willis Reed. But Bellamy doesn't need much spelling when he wants to play ball, and he showed that he wanted to very much when he was traded to the Knicks. Reed shoud become an outstanding rebounding and shooting forward. He has size, strength, skill, and desire. Once he learns to play better defense, particularly in positioning himself, and to work better with Bellamy, there should be no stopping him. The other starting forward, Dave Stallworth, is an excellent freelance ballplayer, very fast and a great ballhandler for a man 6-7. He gets banged around under the boards because of lack of weight but the Knicks can sacrifice rebounding from him with their two big men. Dick Van Arsdale is another comer at forward, small but rugged, and he never gives up. His shooting should improve with experience. Dick Barnett, the team's top guard, needs no work on his shooting. He's outstanding, though he could improve on defense. Howard Komives is a capable defensive guard, a good shooter, and he may yet develop into a playmaker. Actually, the Knicks are hoping their No. 1 draft choice, Cazzie Russell of Michigan, can be a playmaker. He did everything in college and could be a star in his first season. He may be the key to New York's improvement, though this team will be playing together for a whole season for the first time in '66–67 and that alone should spell tremendous improvement. Em Bryant is an ideal man to come off the bench and either harass a hot-shooting opposing guard or hit a few big baskets himself.

BALTIMORE BULLETS: They have been hurt badly by being switched from the weaker division, the West, into the East. The Bullets have also been hurt by the loss of center Johnny Kerr to the Bulls (and to a lesser degree by the loss of Jerry Sloan, who didn't have much chance to develop). The Bullets lack the good big man, like so many teams in the league, and there's just no way to beat the Chamberlains and Russells consistently without a good big man. Bob Ferry and Johnny Kerr did a good job together last season, but Ferry, at 6-8, cannot do it alone. Baltimore does have the deepest set of fine forwards in the league, and coach Mike Farmer will attempt to compensate with them. Gus Johnson and Bailey Howell, both excellent rebounders, are superstars. Many people feel Johnson can still be the best cornerman in the league. Backup men Jim (Bad News) Barnes and Johnny Green are also good board men and capable shooters. Green, in fact, hit .536 per cent of his shots last year. The Bullets have two excellent shooters in the backcourt as well. Don Ohl averaged 20.6 points per game, and Kevin Loughery averaged 18.2 points per game in '65–66. The club's only playmaker is speedy, exciting Johnny Egan. He averaged 9.1 points per game, but because of his size the big forwards tend to shoot over him. Jack Marin, the Bullets' first draft choice, is a fine shooter from Duke and should fill out the backcourt. With Kerr gone, don't be surprised if the 6-8, 240-pound Barnes gets more and more work at center. As we said, Ferry will need help and Barnes is the most likely candidate.

Western Division

LOS ANGELES LAKERS: Three years ago the Lakers offered Henry Finkel a $25,000 two-year contract to sign with them. The 6-11 center from Dayton was then eligible for the draft because his original class had graduated. Well, Finkel's stock has gone down a bit since then. He was still available when it came to LA's second-round draft choice this past spring. Finkel was taken, and he may just help the Lakers on the boards, on defense and as a passing center. Darrall Imhoff and Gene Wiley, each of whom averaged less than five points per game last year, won't do. If Leroy Ellis could only put on about 20 pounds of muscle, he would do nicely. He's a fine shooter, averaging 12.2 points per game in '65–66, but he gets blown away under the backboards. Ellis also has a hard time on defense against the good centers. Fred Schaus's front court is both good and deeper than it's been in many years if Jerry Chambers is the ballplayer he appeared to be at Utah. Chambers was the most-valuable-player in the NCAA tournament and LA's No. 1 draft choice. He will have to develop quickly if the Lakers are to maintain their Western Division dominance. Bob Boozer, a 12.2-points-per-game scorer last year, went to Chicago in the expansion draft. Elgin Baylor and Rudy LaRusso are still around to start at forward. Baylor should be completely recovered from his knee problems and play all year as he played the second half of last season. Schaus lost a solid man from his backcourt to the Bulls, too, in Jim King. But this is the Lakers' deepest position. Jerry West is the best shooting guard in the league, as well as the best money player, and Walt Hazzard came on strong in his second season. Schaus expects Gail Goodrich, who played so well in the playoffs, to keep pace with Hazzard this season.

SAN FRANCISCO WARRIORS: Bill Sharman is fortunate that his first NBA coaching job is with the Warriors at this time. This could be the Western Division's team of the future. In fact, the Warriors should make a strong run at the Lakers this season, providing center Nate Thurmond's back stays well. Nate's sacroiliac troubles have reportedly come from the fact that one of his legs is longer than the other, and all he has to do to avoid problems this season is play with a built-up sneaker. So he should be well, and he is the best center in the West. Rick Barry proved himself to be among the best cornermen as a rookie and will no doubt improve. Fred Hetzel, San Francisco's other No. 1 draft choice of a year ago, got a late start because of injuries but was showing great promise by season's end. Tom Meschery is a hard-nosed forward who averaged 12.8 points per game in '65–66. So the Warriors already seem solid up front. Clyde Lee of Vanderbilt, the team's first draft pick this past spring, is expected to add further depth at the corners. In the backcourt, Guy Rodgers has developed shooting skills to go with his already awesome passing ability. Paul Neumann sat out 14 games with injuries last year, but he's always been a good shooter, better than his 14.4 average indicated. Reserve guard Al Attles is an intelligent, excellent all-round bench man. He has the speed and quickness to drive opponents wild on defense, and he's also a capable shooter (averaging 11.2 points per game and hitting over 50 per cent of his shots from the floor). However, San Francisco could use help in its fourth guard spot. Rookie Steve Vacendec out of Duke may be the answer.

ST. LOUIS HAWKS: This is a team without a real superstar, but it has a nucleus of fine ballplayers who work well together. Seven Hawk players scored in double figures last season, which is what you'd call a balanced attack, and that's been Boston's secret for many years. Center Zelmo Beaty had by far his best season, averaging 20.7 points per game and pulling down 1,086 rebounds. The man who helped him most on the boards is underrated Bill Bridges, a tough 6-6 cornerman. He'll probably never be a great shooter (hitting just over 40 per cent of his shots in compiling a 13.0 average), but he's the kind of player coaches like because he doesn't quit (951 rebounds). Joe Caldwell, the other starting forward, had some adjustment problems in Detroit that he seems to have resolved. Only 6-5, he more than makes up for his lack of height with his acrobatic jumping ability. The implication last season was that Cliff Hagan was going to retire, but this hasn't been confirmed.

If he returns, he'll be a part-time player at most. The Hawks surprised many people by keeping veteran forward Gene Tormohlen over young Jim Washington in the expansion draft. They must know something the rest of us don't. Tormohlen is generally regarded as a journeyman ballplayer while Washington appears to have a chance to develop into a solid forward. The Hawks were also hurt in their backcourt depth by the loss of Jeff Mullins to Chicago. This is undoubtedly why coach Richie Guerin has been persuaded to remain a player for another year. He may not have to if top draft choices Lou Hudson of Minnesota and Dick Snyder of Davidson play up to their potential. Hudson, particularly, appears to be a can't-miss. Lenny Wilkens is, of course, the backcourt leader of the Hawks. A fine all-round ballplayer, he averaged 18.0 points per game last season. Ron Thorn could be almost as good if he'd relax and play his game; he has the ability.

DETROIT PISTONS: Despite three fine ballplayers, the Pistons are a team with multiple problems. Dave DeBusschere and Ray Scott are top cornermen, with Scott being the better shooter and DeBusschere being the better all-round performer. And Eddie Miles is a first-rate shooting guard (19.6-points-per-game average last season), though no one should spend much time waiting for him to pass to them. Tom Van Arsdale, like his twin brother Dick in New York, is a very capable swing man, but he just doesn't seem to have the skills to play back regularly or the size to play forward regularly. Chico Vaughn has shown that he can shoot from the backcourt, but the only trouble is that he stays injured so much that he's really not much help to a team. The other Detroit players are mediocre. DeBusschere has said Reggie Harding will never play for the team as long as he's around. However, Harding has been cleared by the courts and if the Pistons are to get back into contention, Harding may well be their only chance. He's a seven-foot center who can do at least an adequate job—and no other Piston center can make that statement. DeBusschere is hoping his No. 2 draft choice, Dorrie Murray out of the University of Detroit, Dave's alma mater, rises to the challenge. One draft choice the Pistons don't have to worry about is Dave Bing of Syracuse. Lightning fast, a terrific shooter, and able playmaker, Bing may make

Detroit fans forgive the team for losing Cazzie Russell to New York on a coin toss. The Pistons did get another Michigan player to go with Bill Buntin, Oliver Darden. Unfortunately, Darden had a very average senior season in college and may be just another Buntin.

CHICAGO BULLS: When Johnny Kerr met the press after being named coach of the National Basketball Association's newest franchise, he named the men he would start if he had to put a lineup on the floor that day. They were Bob Boozer and Jim Washington at the corners, Nate Bowman at center, and Jim King and Jerry Sloan at the guards. Boozer and King were substitutes with the Los Angeles Lakers, Washington was a sub with the Hawks, Sloan was a sub with the Bullets and Bowman was a Cincinnati Royal draft choice who didn't even make the team. He was farmed out. He's young, though, and could develop, along with Sloan, Washington, Jeff Mullins (from St. Louis), Barry Clemens (a good shooter from New York), and McCoy McClemore (who brings potentially good all-round skills from San Francisco). Other Bull draftees from the older teams were John Thompson and Ron Bonham (Boston), Gerry Ward and Al Bianchi (Philadelphia), Tom Thacker (Cincinnati), Len Chappell (New York), Keith Erickson (San Francisco), and Don Kojis and Jim Barnhill (Detroit). Chicago's one bright spot was its top college draft choice, Dave Schellhase, the high-scorer from Purdue. Kerr also has said, "We've discussed many new things we may try in our system. For one thing, we may attempt platooning, keeping five fresh players in a game at all times." He'll definitely have to try something, and may very well end up as the league's fourth player-coach this season.

LEW ALCINDOR

When Lew Alcindor was at Power Memorial High School in New York City he established a reputation as (1) the greatest high-school player in the country, perhaps of all time, and (2) the most inaccessible high-school player in the country, definitely of all time.

Now, probably this was a very good thing for young Lew. From the time the 7-1½-inch Alcindor was a sophomore at Power, college coaches all over the United States knew he was going to be something beyond all ordinary basketball superstars. In fact, during Lew's junior year, New York Knickerbocker coach Eddie Donovan, who is now the team's general manager, said: "Alcindor's the best high-school player I've ever seen. He could step right into my lineup right now." Remember, this was *six years* before Alcindor would even be eligible to be drafted by a National Basketball Association team. And here was a professional coach saying Lew was already capable of playing in the NBA.

In other words, Alcindor was getting so much publicity that Power Coach Jack Donohue certainly did the boy no harm when he refused to allow anyone to interview him, refused to allow college coaches to talk to him. So many people were after Lew that, had he attempted to see even a portion of them, his B-plus average likely would have been affected. So the youngster might have suffered had not Donohue held fast to the rule he'd instituted for his players when he'd taken the coaching job at Power five years before Lew's arrival.

However, a man in the limelight, even a young man like Alcindor, does have obligations to meet eventually. Not only to the public but to himself. He can't say, "Talk to the coach" forever. No one has a coach all his life.

When Lew reached college everyone automatically assumed that his years of silence would be over. The press couldn't wait to see him in his first game and to interview him afterward.

Well, Alcindor's first game with the UCLA freshman team was a memorable one, because the frosh played the varsity, and the varsity had won the National Collegiate Athletic Association championship the year before. The national champions had lost Gail Goodrich to graduation, but this was still a very fine college team. It so happened that the frosh, led by Alcindor, were a better team.

Lew scored 31 points, pulled down 21 rebounds and blocked seven shots as the freshmen won, 75-60. But afterward, no one could find out for publication what he thought of his performance. No one could find out what he thought about the transition from high-school to college basketball. No one could find out what he thought about the Beatles, Vietnam, ice cream sodas, or tall fruggers. No one could find out anything from Alcindor because once again he was surrounded by a no-interviews rule.

"It's my rule," athletic director J.D. Morgan announced with a straight face. "It's been in existence since I became athletic director here. The press is not permitted to talk to any freshman athlete, not only Lew."

That sounds reasonable enough in an unreasonable way. Because the fact is that in J.D. Morgan's three years as athletic director at UCLA, no one from the press ever had any trouble interviewing a freshman athlete before Alcindor.

"This is a very tough school," Morgan further explained, or rationalized. "The freshman year is the most difficult and we don't want anything to interfere with Lew's studies. I owe that to him and to his parents."

Wouldn't it have been more reasonable to permit Alcindor to be interviewed and—when and if the interviews seemed to be interfering with his studies—then issue the press-off-limits rule? Phil Pepe, the fine New York newspaper columnist who has known Lew Alcindor for a half-dozen years, thinks so. Pepe wrote in the *World-Telegram and Sun* last January about a Friday night in Fullerton, California, that was like no other ever for the people in that town. Four thousand and 300 people swelled the new gym to overflowing that night because Lew Alcindor was playing basketball there for the first time.

"They came for the same reason they would go see Jo-Jo the Dog-Faced Boy, or Matilda the Fat Lady, or Igor the Sword Swallower," Pepe wrote. "They came to snicker and sneer and gawk at this unusual young man who would like to run and hide from the snickerers, the sneerers and the gawkers, but knows he cannot. When they introduced him it was not 'Lewis Alcindor of UCLA,' it was 'Lewis Alcindor, seven feet, one-and-one-half inches,' and they introduced him right after Lucius Allen, who is 6-2, and Lew had to run out on the court with all those eyes staring at him, and he had to stand next to Lucius Allen and listen to the crowd buzz and snicker and laugh."

Pepe went on to point out that it was not a basketball game but an exhibition. Lew Alcindor was on exhibition, a young man who was regarded by the people in attendance as a freak to be held in awe.

"They are doing Lewis Alcindor a great disservice," Pepe wrote. "He is not a freak and he is not an ogre. I have known him for six years and I have had several long discussions with him. And I have found him to be an unusually intelligent, unusually sensitive young man in addition to being probably the greatest prospect in the history of basketball. These are the things the people of Southern California do not know about Alcindor because UCLA has put an impenetrable wall of security around him."

Right. No one knows what his interests are, what his beliefs are, what his feelings are. No one has been able to ask him. When Pepe tried, he got through to Lew, who said, "If it's for an interview, I'm sorry, but I'll have to say no." Pepe said he did not believe Lew wanted it that way, but that was the rule.

UCLA's varsity coach, Johnny Wooden, says, "Lew wants it this way and I'm glad. We want the boy to develop normally and he can't do that if he's interviewed every day of the week."

This is patently nonsense. No one wants to interview anyone every day of the week, not even the Beatles, of whom there are four. And certainly it is not normal for a teenager to be denied the right to speak for himself, to let people know that despite the fact that he happens to be tall and a good athlete that he is also a human being with character and a personality.

Certainly he is a lot of basketball player, as he showed

his freshman year. In his final game of the season Lew played with a slash on his left hand which required four stitches. Yet he scored 35 points and grabbed 25 rebounds as the UCLA frosh beat the USC frosh, 108-74. It was the 17th time in 21 games that the UCLA frosh had scored over 100 points. It was also their 21st win in 21 games.

Alcindor was the big reason but by no means the only reason this team was so good. It featured three other high-school All-Americas—Lucius Allen of Kansas City, Kenny Heitz of Santa Maria, and Lynn Shackelford of Burbank. They scored 22, 20, and 17 points, respectively, in that last game.

Overall, Alcindor averaged 33 points a game as the frosh team averaged 113.5 points per game while holding opponents to a 59.7 average. Coach Gary Cunningham summarized Lew's freshman season by saying, "When Alcindor came to us he was a great offensive player. We tried to give him a few more moves. For example, we worked on his left hand, trying to give him a lefthanded hook. At first Lew had a tendency to hold the ball when he took it off the board. Now he has a quicker release, passing out right away."

It was the lowest-key report we'd ever seen on Alcindor. Bill Sharman, the former Boston Celtic star who will coach the San Francisco Warriors this season, saw Lew play one game last year and said he could play in the NBA immediately. What's more, Sharman said Alcindor could be worth more than $100,000 a year to an NBA team.

Marv Harsham, the varsity coach at Washington State, shook his head in disbelief after seeing Alcindor in action. "What can you say?" Harsham said. "Alcindor is simply great. He can hold you off with one hand and put the ball in the basket with the other."

The growing reports on his ability go on and on. Yet all last season reports of Alcindor's dissatisfaction at UCLA went on and on, too. Insiders claimed Lew was sorry he chose the West Coast school after all. But, again, nobody'll find out until they talk to Lew. Perhaps the fact that he's not allowed to talk is part of the dissatisfaction.

DICK BARNETT

For Dick Barnett, the 1965–66 National Basketball Association season was both his greatest and his most disappointing. But Barnett has known so much frustration in his six-year NBA career that he accepted this year's disappointment calmly even if he was hurt deeply inside.

The great part of the season began for Dick just before the first game. Barnett, who had spent the last three seasons in the shadows of Jerry West and Elgin Baylor with the Los Angeles Lakers, was traded to the New York Knickerbockers. Although he had averaged over 18 points a game for Los Angeles in two of his seasons there, Dick was seldom used as a starter and this bothered him. He was overjoyed with the trade. He knew he would not only be a starter with New York, but that he would have a chance to demonstrate his superstar scoring abilities that had always been held back by the Laker style.

The Knicks were, of course, even happier than Dick. During the previous season only one New York guard had averaged in double figures, young Howie Komives. Knick coach Harry Gallatin said, "The other clubs won't be able to cheat on our backcourt anymore." Gallatin went on to point out that Barnett would also take the pressure off New York's front court, which was strong enough to give up one of its members for Dick. That was 6–8 former Kansas All-America Bob Boozer, who averaged 13.1 points per game through two seasons with the Knicks.

Barnett wasted no time in showing New York fans what he could do with a basketball. He immediately established himself as a potential 40-point-plus scorer on any given night. Knick fans had no idea the 6-4 guard from Tennessee A & I was that dangerous, though they should have. As the Lakers' sixth man Dick had demonstrated his hot shooting ability on many occasions. One season in which he averaged 18 points a game he scored more than 30 points in seven games, more than 35 points in five games.

So when a New York writer asked Barnett some two months into the season how he could explain his almost 30-points-per-game average, Dick patiently said, "If you are a shooter, which I think I am, then the amount you score depends mostly on the number of shots you take. Here, in New York, I'm less inhibited."

The Knicks, of course, had no Jerry West or Elgin Baylor. They did have Walt Bellamy, but he was an inside threat. Barnett was the outside threat and was expected to shoot a lot. He always has hit a very fine percentage of his shots (.469 this past season). Dick reveled in his new opportunity to fire away at will.

"It's quite a challenge to me here," he said, "but I can't say I'm not enjoying it. Of course, if you score 40 points and don't win a ball game, it isn't as much fun as scoring 20 and winning. But the way I figure it, if I can get 40 we stand a good chance of winning."

Almost invariably when the Knicks won, Barnett was the scoring leader. Unfortunately, when it came time to vote for the NBA All-Star team, some rival coaches were not impressed by Dick's scoring. He did not make the team and that was his big disappointment. He justifiably felt the lack of justice when he, averaging 29 points a game, was left off the team in favor of Cincinnati guard Adrian Smith, averaging 19 points a game at the time. "Would I call it a raw deal?" Dick repeated the question. "Yeah, that's just what it is. I'm not just disappointed . . . I feel it's a raw deal."

Here's how it happened. Eight members of the ten-man East team were selected by sportswriters and broadcasters. The guards named were Oscar Robertson, Sam Jones, and Hal Greer. Even though Barnett was outscoring all of them except Robertson, there was no cause for alarm because the four Eastern coaches were to vote another guard onto the team, and Barnett seemed a lock. Only Smith got three votes. Knick coach Dick McGuire (who had replaced Gallatin) naturally voted for Barnett. Cincinnati coach Jack McMahon naturally voted for his player, Smith. Why Boston coach Red Auerbach voted for Smith nobody knows. Philadelphia coach Dolph Schayes said, "I think there's too much emphasis on scoring. Well, Smith plays defense, too. I know he kills us. Barnett had only played one game against us at the time I voted—last week—and that's the only way I can judge."

"That's bull about Smith killing Philly," one writer who covers the 76ers told *Newsday*'s Joe Donnelly. "He has scored well, but only because Dolph tells the team to concentrate on Oscar and that Smith, even with 25 points, isn't going to hurt them. The whole thing is implausible."

It was implausible to Hawks coach Richie Guerin and Bullets coach Paul Seymour, too. Said Guerin: "There's no way you can leave Barnett off that team. He's having a better year than any of the East guards except Oscar. I can understand McMahon; it was a sentimental vote. But what tbout those other guys?"

Said Seymour: "They've got to be kidding to leave Barnett off. Tell Dick he's the better player," Paul told a New York writer. "Tell him I thought he should have been an All-Star."

Dick himself thought so. "They're supposed to go on the effort of this season. Statistically speaking, I think my record is better than Sam Jones's and Hal Greer's this season—not even to mention Adrian Smith.

"My history throughout my NBA career has always been something like this. Being on that All-Star team was a goal, but not being on it wasn't a shock. I thought I should have made it twice before. But nobody ever made it as a sub before [John] Havlicek. When I came to New York this season as a starter I thought I could make it. If I didn't make it this season, I don't think I'll ever make it."

He doesn't really believe that, but he does feel most people weren't aware of his talent when he was a sixth man with the Lakers. Los Angeles fans did. They loved his unique shooting style and cheered wildly every time Dick bounced off the bench. A lefthander, Barnett fires his jump shot on a line rather than a conventional arc. He jumps, kicks his heels under his butt and pops. Up until he joined the Knicks he yelled, "Fall back, baby," and that became his nickname. The cry was a signal to teammates that they needn't charge for the rebound but should fall back on defense. The shot, in other words, was in the moment it left his hands. "Fall back, baby," became the rallying cry of Laker fans whenever Dick appeared on court.

Barnett was known as a great kidder with the Lakers, a flashy dresser, and a man about town until he married a couple of years ago. "When the crowd cheers him," Bill Libby reported in *Sport* Magazine, "Dick seems about to rush into the stands to kiss each fan, as Goose Tatum might do. He calls everyone and everything darlin'. 'Wasn't that a darlin' shot?' he will say after a brilliant basket. 'Wasn't that a darlin' shot?' he will say after a missed basket. It's all in the way he sees it. He is a droll fellow."

But when he joined the Knicks Barnett was more subdued, saying, "That was my Los Angeles period. Now that I'm in New York, I may decide to change my entire personality."

The thing he changed most was his status, from excellent sixth man to superstar. "Even a kid on a grade-school team wants to be a starter," Dick said when he was with the Lakers. "I see ten guys out there, I have to figure I'm as good as some of them. I don't mind the way I've been used. But I can't help thinking I could do more for my team and more for myself if I was a regular. So I want to be a regular. Regulars get rich. I'd like to get rich."

A No. 1 draft choice of the old Syracuse Nationals in 1959, Dick averaged 12 points per game as a rookie playing behind Larry Costello and Hal Greer. Used more frequently the next year, he averaged 16.9 points a game. But he still wasn't a regular and "was disenchanted," he says. He asked to be traded. The Lakers tried to acquire him then. When the deal fell through, Barnett jumped to the new American Basketball League. He was a star but still wasn't happy. When Syracuse sold him to the Lakers, he signed with them for a very nice salary.

Despite his heroics in Los Angeles, though, he never attained the stardom he felt he could earn as a starter. Laker coach Fred Schaus once said, "Barnett is at least an All-Star, but he has not made the All-Star team because he has the label of a sub, which is unfair. This has become a game in which it is very important for a team to have a star like Barnett ready on the bench."

Schaus kept him on the bench because two great shooters don't complement each other in the same backcourt.

But the Knicks have only one, and his name is Barnett. He slumped as a result of injuries at the end of his first season in New York and still averaged 23.1 points per game. This season you get bet Dick Barnett will make the All-Star team. He's finally on the way to becoming rich.

RICK BARRY

Early in his first season in the National Basketball Association, Rick Barry was had. Barry, a 6-7, 205-pound All-America from the University of Miami, had won the NCAA scoring championship the previous season with a 37.4-points-per-game average. But this was the NBA and on this night against the Baltimore Bullets, the slim young man from Roselle Park, New Jersey, learned what it was like to be worked over by a pro. Ben Warley, the Bullet who was guarding him, bounced Barry, bumped Barry, banged Barry, elbowed Barry, and generally shoved him all over the court.

Said Warley afterwards: "I all but stuffed him in the basket."

Warley is a hard-nosed veteran, but he had never been accused of throwing his weight around before. Simply because Ben has no weight. Warley is slightly shorter and slightly lighter even than Barry. And the concern about Barry as a pro was always whether he could stand up to the punishment through an 80-game schedule. The average NBA cornerman weighs between 225 and 240 pounds. Here Barry had been black-and-blued by a 200-pounder . . . what would he do against a guy like Dave DeBusschere, for example?

DeBusschere, the Detroit Piston player-coach, is a 6-6, 225-pounder who plays a clean but tough game of basketball. Dave often outrebounds bigger men and shuts off their scoring ability on the strength of his determination and rugged approach to the game.

In Barry's first meeting with DeBusschere he learned another lesson in NBA play. DeBusschere held Rick to eight points and said later: "Barry should send away for some muscles. He can't push you out of the way, so he has to go around you. And we don't think he's that fast or maneuverable."

Dave, it turned out, was a bit hasty in his judgment. The Warriors played the Pistons again a week later and after this game DeBusschere was biting his tongue. In less than 30 minues, Barry scored 23 points on him. Rick showed that he had more than enough quickness and maneuverability to get open for shots and to get them off for baskets. Barry soon proved that he belonged in the NBA, and his thin build and boyish face no doubt actually contributed to his success.

"High-school kids look older than him and you tend to relax a little playing him," Dave Gambee of the Philadelphia 76ers. "First time I did that he had 22 points off me *in two periods*. He may be skinny, but once he has his hands on the ball, you don't get it away from him. He has great hands."

Frank Mieuli, the Warrior owner, said all that talk about Barry's lack of bulk was a lot of nonsense, as far as he was concerned. "They talk as if we paid Rick as much money [estimated $30,000 bonus and salary his first season] as we've ever paid anyone except Wilt Chamberlain and then suddenly discovered he was frail," Mieuli said. "Malarkey. Here's an athlete who's played maybe 400 games in his life and never had an injury. He's not frail. Compare him to Tom Meschery on our club, who's a brute of a man. In four pro years and four college years, Meschery's had only one season when he didn't have a busted jaw or some other crippling injury.

"The same goes for many 'tough' types. Barry's as flexible as a whip and a long time ago, when we scouted him in competition against the Russian national team, we saw how he reacts when somebody challenges him."

The Warriors first scouted Barry at the College All-Star game in Kentucky when general manager Bob Ferrick was preparing his draft list. "We knew he could score points," Ferrick said afterwards, "but that was all we were sure of. Alex Hannum went to the All-Star game in person, and I saw it on television, and we both came away feeling that the kid had what it takes. He got in there and mixed it up with the best in the country and came out looking great. He's strong, quick, and, as I said, he can *can* shoot."

Hannum, who coached at San Francisco until he was

fired at the end of last season and signed on with Philadelphia, also scouted Barry against the Russians. Alex
reported that Nicolai Volnov, the big, strong star of the
USSR team, got rough with Barry and Rick quickly re-
taliated. "He began to hit on drives, on jumpers, on hooks,
from everywhere, and ran up 14 points," Hannum said.
"The Americans won in overtime because of Rick, and we
knew we had a draft choice who could take care of himself."

Rick had his early problems, but they were short-lived.
He found ways to take care of himself besides simply
making his opponent look bad by scoring all over him. In
a game against the Celtics Rick was involved in a scramble
for a ball near the sideline. Suddenly a Celtic dropped to
the floor in pain. "All I did," Barry calmly explained
later, "was try to bank the ball off his knee so it would
bounce out of bounds and we'd get possession."

Teammate Guy Rodgers, seated nearby in the locker
room, laughed. "Yes," said Rodgers, "but it seems you got
the ball a little high and caught that boy right in the
belly."

Harry Gallatin, then coaching the Knicks, was one of
the first opposing coaches to tab Barry a star. Rick not
only scored 33 points against New York in an early
game, but was outstanding in controlling the offensive
boards. Said Gallatin: "He looks like he could be a real
star, maybe a superstar."

Other NBA coaches were soon agreeing with Gallatin,
including the man who replaced him as coach, Dick
McGuire. Said McGuire: "The kid is just great. When you
think he's getting tired, he's by you and has two points."

Said Cincinnati's Jack McMahon: "He sure knows why
the hoop is up there. He has more moves toward getting
two points than any rookie I have seen in a long time."

Said Boston's Red Auerbach: "He knows how to get
the ball—and he knows what to do with it after he gets
it."

Said Barry's own coach, Alex Hannum: "One big plus
about Rick is that he is never satisfied. After every game,
even when he scores 40 points, he will go home and think
about the shot he missed and then go to practice and work
on it so he won't miss it again." Alex smiled. "Heck, Rick
could be the first player never to miss a shot."

In early April Barry became the highest-scoring rookie forward in the history of the NBA. Elgin Baylor held the previous record, having scored 1,739 points in 69 games as a rookie. When Rick was told about his feat he said, "What record?" He knew nothing about it. In fact, he didn't even seem impressed with his play, saying, "I'm fortunate to be scoring, but I'm not pleased with my shooting. I still miss too many from outside."

To a degree this was true. Rick is not a great outside shooter, but he is a good one. What's more, he is outstanding at following his own shots and those of teammates to get the "garbage" underneath the basket. Picking off the "garbage" is nothing but hard work, hustle, and desire.

Barry has always been a hard worker on a basketball court, in high school and at Miami under coach Bruce Hale. In college Rick worked hard to impress not only Hale but Hale's daughter Pamela, whom Barry married after graduation.

Then he began his NBA career, with an admitted certain amount of trepidation because of his lack of weight. But it turned out to be a problem that he could and did overcome by hard work. And when the annual NBA All-Star team was voted by the league writers and broadcasters at mid-season, Rick Barry was the lone rookie on the team. He was selected to the first team, too.

At season's end another All-Star team was voted and again Barry was named to the first team. In addition, the coaches selected a Rookie All-Star team at season's end. Barry was the only unanimous choice. Naturally he was Rookie-of-the-Year, becoming only the fourth man in league history to score over 2,000 points in his first season. Rick had 2,059, a 25.7-points-per-game average.

"Some of the scouts," Barry remarked at the time, "said I couldn't make it in the National Basketball Association because of my size. I was determined to prove they were wrong."

ELGIN BAYLOR

In recent years, Elgin Baylor of the Los Angeles Lakers has known considerable frustration in trying to play professional basketball. The 6-5, 225-pound All-Star's troubles began during the 1961–62 NBA season. He was recalled by the Army during the Berlin Crisis and got into only 48 of 80 league games that season. Two years later calcium deposits on his knees reduced him to only half the player he had been, and many people thought he was on the way out of the NBA.

But Baylor made a magnificent recovery from knee treatments in the off-season and came back strong in '64–65. He averaged 27.1 points per game and 12.8 rebounds per game. He was also ninth in the league in assists with 280, a very high total for a forward. Elgin Baylor was once again one of the most exciting players ever to play pro basketball, driving, leaping, hanging in the air, and flipping the ball into the basket from all angles.

However, in the opening playoff game against the Baltimore Bullets, Baylor's career appeared to be ended. "It was a fluke thing," Elgin recalled early this past season. "I went up for a jump shot and when I came down, my left foot felt weak, like it was going to give way under me. But I kept running up and down the floor until the pain got too great and I went to the bench. X-rays showed that I had torn part of my kneecap away, and I was operated on the next day."

The man who performed the operation was Dr. Robert Kerlan of Los Angeles, the man who had saved the pitching career of Sandy Koufax when the Dodger superstar came down with an arthritic elbow. But even after the surgery, experts felt Baylor would never play pro basketball again. Laker general manager Lou Mohs consulted several other leading bone specialists as to Elgin's future.

33

"They agreed," said Mohs, "that the odds against his playing pro ball again were about 99 to 1. They felt that it would not be possible to attach the tendons in such a way as to permit complete freedom of movement."

The doctors had no way of knowing about Baylor's great pride, though. Dr. Kerlan gave him careful instructions, and Elgin followed them carefully. Whenever Elgin got discouraged, his wife Ruby stepped in and encouraged him. And gradually the knee began to respond to therapy.

"Every day except Saturday and Sunday I worked out from 8:30 in the morning," Baylor recalled, "until 2:30 in the afternoon. I went down to the L.A. High School and ran around the stadium for an hour and spent most of the time running up and down the stairs. After that I'd get whirlpool treatments in the doctor's office and then I'd go home and lift weights, skip rope, and shoot baskets in my backyard. I tried riding a bike out in the hills, but the traffic got to be too much and I had to stop or get run over."

Despite the dedication to making a comeback, when the National Basketball Association season opened in mid-October Baylor was playing with a limp, and on a part-time basis. Said Laker coach Fred Schaus: "Dr. Kerlan told us not to rush it. Elgin hasn't played more than 33 minutes in our exhibition games. We are bringing him along gradually to a plateau where he could be ready to go all out by November, December, or January 1. There is no way of telling right now."

There was no way of telling if Baylor would ever regain even a portion of his old skills. And as late as mid-December people were still wondering about Baylor. There was a game in New York, for example, with the Knicks leading the Lakers by four points with two-and-a-half minutes to play. Suddenly Schaus sent in substitute Jim King . . . for Elgin Baylor. Jim King for Elgin Baylor with time running out and the game on the line? "He's finished," said Tom Panagakos, summing up the feeling of the majority in Madison Square Garden that night. And anything Tom Panagakos says about professional basketball is not to be taken lightly. A former all-city player himself, Panagakos never misses a game at the Garden, and he often turns out to be more perceptive than the coaches around the league. He may be the top amateur basketball expert in the country and here he was saying, "Baylor still gets that great rebound position, but he can't get off the floor. A 6-5 forward's got to be able to jump and the spring's gone from Baylor's legs. Would you ever believe Schaus would send in Jim King for Elgin Baylor?"

But in the locker room after the game, Baylor wasn't concerned. He said the knee was slowly but surely coming back despite the fact that at the moment he was still struggling. "I am relying strictly on what Dr. Kerlan has told me. The knee took quite a while to come around after they took the cast off. But it did and I've had no trouble with it since then." The thing that was bothering him then, Elgin said, was a strained tendon. He'd incurred that the previous month when, banged in mid-air while rebounding, he'd twisted it.

Yet reporters weren't convinced, and they pressed Baylor for signs from him that he might be on the way out. Elgin didn't believe that, but he said when the time comes for him to quit he would be ready. "I think I'm prepared for it," he said, meaning mentally as well as financially. "I have a travel agency in LA and I'm going to start boys' basketball camps in Arthur, Washington, and in Los Angeles this summer."

He maintained, though, that he wasn't finished. And then he proceeded to prove it. In a game against the Bullets on February 9, Baylor played his longest stretch of the season —45 minutes—scored 28 points, and had five assists. He was the difference in the Laker victory. Afterwards Schaus said, "Elgin's knees are all right now; it's just a matter of getting them strengthened. We tried to use him as much as possible earlier in the season even though it hurt us because we knew he needed the work to come back. But for the past three or four weeks he's been helping us a lot. If he doesn't have any more setbacks (like the strained tendon), he should be all right. We're going to need him in the stretch."

They had him in the stretch. Baylor wasn't all the way back (nobody could be from the delicate operation he had), but you couldn't prove it to the Knicks on March 8. New York beat Los Angeles in Madison Square Garden that night, 133-132 in overtime. The Knicks couldn't stop Baylor, though. Elgin scored 46 points, took down 17 rebounds and had five assists in 45 minutes of action. The

Knicks tried several different defenders and ever conceivable trick to harass Baylor—hitting him, shoving him, hanging on him. Nothing worked.

"It's quite a tribute to a guy to fight his way back," Schaus said, "when everyone just about kissed him off. Except for Elgin himself. He has so much pride."

Actually, Elgin made a bad pass that cost LA the game when New York's Dave Stallworth intercepted. "I saw Stallworth sneaking in," Elgin said, "and I tried to pull the ball back. But it slipped and sailed in the air."

Schaus wasn't even upset. He was too happy to have Baylor looking like the old Baylor once more. He was an important factor in the Lakers' drive for another title, taking some of the pressure off Jerry West, who had carried the team most of the season. And in the playoffs Baylor continued to be sensational.

In the April 3 game against St. Louis, Baylor scored 42 points and set an NBA field goal record for playoff competition with 819, passing former Celtic star Tommy Heinsohn. Los Angeles won the game, 125-116, and St. Louis coach Richie Guerin said, "Baylor was the difference. He made the clutch shots when they had to be made. I never thought he could play this kind of basketball after his serious knee operation last year."

Nobody did, really, except for Dr. Robert Kerlan and a guy named Baylor who had overcome other frustrations in the past and who wasn't about to let this one end his career. He'll decide when he's ready to quit. As everyone says, he has too much pride to do otherwise.

WALT BELLAMY

Since its beginnings in 1946, the National Basketball Association lived by a maxim: If you have a good big man who, for one reason or another, does not get along with your coach—fire your coach. He may be a very excellent coach, a lover of dogs and small children, but if he can't get along with your center, dump him. There are a great many coaches in this world. There are very few good big men. So keep going through coaches until you find one who can get along with, and get something out of, your good big man.

However, this maxim was shattered midway through the 1964–65 season when Wilt Chamberlain was traded. And the maxim may have been buried for good last season when Walt Bellamy was traded by the Baltimore Bullets to the New York Knickerbockers. Chamberlain, Bellamy, and Bill Russell of Boston are the three outstanding big men in the league. Two were traded, and the other was named coach of his team, which is another solution to the problem of center and coach banging heads (though this certainly was never the case with Russell and Red Auerbach).

There was no questioning Bellamy's offensive ability. He had led the Bullets (who started in Chicago) in scoring and rebounding for all five years of their existence. But during the '64–65 season the Bullets were sold to a new group of owners, Arnie Heft, Abe Pollin, and Earl Foreman. Heft, a likable, outspoken fellow, is a basketball fan. Although he had become a wealthy contractor, he continued to referee in the NBA until a few years ago. He loves basketball, and he loves to see it played well. After he bought the Bullets he decided Walt Bellamy was not playing up to his potential, and he let people know about this.

Therefore it was no surprise when Walter was traded. First, Heft had sent Bellamy a new contract calling for a pay cut and Walt became a holdout. "Sure we offered Bellamy a pay cut," Heft said at the time. "Why not? Didn't we have to fine him for loafing last year? Didn't we bench him for a half dozen games? Didn't he let us down in the playoffs, letting Gene Wiley of the Lakers eat him up? When you have that kind of year, you've got to expect a pay cut."

Bellamy did not expect a pay cut. Especially when Russell and Chamberlain had recently signed $100,000 contracts. Walt supposedly ranked just below them, yet he had made $30,000 the previous season and now he was being asked to accept $25,000. Bellamy didn't know whether his two rivals had actually received those huge salaries, but he did see Chamberlain at the annual Maurice Stokes benefit game at Kutscher's Country Club in August and he said, "Wilt was really happy, happier than I've ever seen him. Whatever his raise—whether it was 97 cents or $20,000—he's happy. That's all I want, a salary that will give me peace of mind."

Finally a compromise was reached and Bellamy reported to the Bullets late in the exhibition season. Walt seemed reasonably satisfied and said he was looking forward to playing under new coach Paul Seymour. Buddy Jeannette, who as coach the previous year had fined Bellamy and benched him for eight games, had moved up to become general manager. "I talked to Seymour and he told me he has complete confidence in me," Bellamy said. "I liked that. Nobody ever told me that before here."

The confidence didn't last when the Bullets got off to a losing start. Seymour had Bellamy on the bench at the beginning of the seventh game of the season. "According to statistics," Seymour explained after Baltimore lost again, "Bellamy can score just as much when he plays a shorter time. I made it clear before that I have no permanent starting lineup. I might bench anybody. Bellamy didn't say a word, and he was the loudest guy [cheering on teammates] on the bench."

Bellamy still played 24 minutes that night, scored ten points, and grabbed 13 rebounds, but it hurt him not to start even though he didn't show it. The 6-10 center from New Bern, North Carolina, is not the type of guy to show his emotions. He is shy, quiet, and not particularly articulate. But he is sensitive, and he feels deeply. It pained him not to start when he knew his skills were far superior to those of 33-year-old Johnny Kerr, who played ahead of him.

It hurt him, too, shortly thereafter when he was traded. It is a blow to any athlete when he is traded the first time because he feels he is being rejected by the team getting rid of him. When Bellamy reported to New York, Harry Gallatin was still coaching the Knicks, and he and Walt talked. They agreed that Bellamy could be a big star in New York, that it was a real opportunity for him, and that it was up to him to make the most of it.

Ironically, Bellamy's first game with the Knicks was against his former team in Baltimore. Walt played a very average game, which is to be expected from a man joining teammates whose patterns and skills are a bit strange to him. And afterwards in the locker room, Walt had to be admired. He answered reporters' questions calmly and refused to lash out at his critics in Baltimore. Buddy Jeannette had called him "irresponsible and unreachable—you just can't communicate with him."

But Walt said, "I don't think I got a bum rap. I have no criticism to make, no animosity against anyone in Baltimore. I had some wonderful relationships here, and remember, I have a home here, so I wouldn't have stayed here if I didn't like the city."

Bellamy did tell Milton Gross of the New York *Post* that before he came to New York, no coach had ever impressed him with the need to play defense. This seemed hardly likely, yet it is possible that no other pro coach had been able to communicate this information to Bellamy. This would, if true, have to be considered a lack in his coaches.

"Somebody's got to make you aware of defense," Walt said, "but nobody ever did. I came into the pros five years ago and had a big start as a scorer [averaging almost 32 points a game with an impossibly bad expansion team]. You become conscious of points, and it's the thing you want to keep doing, but I've never been selfish, as they say. They had to say something about me. They can't say I'm running around. They can't say I'm staying out in the streets. They can't say I'm a bad guy. They can't say that every time the ball came to me it would stop, and I would go up for a shot. There never was a situation where I was hogging the ball or doing something they didn't want me to do."

Obviously he wasn't doing what was expected of him or he wouldn't have been traded, even for three fine players like Jim Barnes, Johnny Green, and Johnny Egan. None of them is a 6-10 center who is an extremely accurate outside shooter. Since there is no meanness in Walt Bellamy, perhaps communication was the whole problem. He never really knew what was expected of him, and he always seemed to figure things would work out for the best eventually.

This attitude stems from his background. Walt was raised by his grandmother, a very religious woman who was highly respected. "She was a pillar of the community," he says. "She worked as a domestic, but she worked for the mayor." An aunt also helped raise him, and he has the greatest respect for these ladies and was deeply influenced by them.

"My aunt and my grandmother brought out the true values of life," Walt says. "I am easy-going; I can adjust to any situation. I was raised in a church-sponsored home. Things don't particularly disturb me. I don't like them said about me and I don't like to lose, but these things are going to happen. You say to yourself, 'Tomorrow will be a new day.' "

Perhaps the new day arrived when Walt reached New York. He had his troubles at first. The entire Knick team was remade, with two rookies, two second-year men, and two men who were new to the team, Bellamy and Dick Barnett, doing most of the playing. But the team slowly began to jell and by February New York general manager Eddie Donovan was very pleased with his trade. "Walt looks like he is beginning to feel at home. It's like I said when we made the trade—we didn't care what others said about him; all we cared about was what he did for us."

Veteran Tom Gola said, "It's nice to be with a club that's winning a few. Give the credit to the big guy, Walt Bellamy. He's really pulling the club together. He even picks up little guys coming down court on the fast break."

Maybe Bellamy will cause that don't-trade-your-big-man maxim to be reinstated. Next season will be the tell.

WILT CHAMBERLAIN

Perhaps Wilt Chamberlain is doomed to being ever involved in controversy and frustration. Just when you think he's shaken it at last, he pops right back into the middle of one.

When the 1965–66 regular season ended, for example, it appeared as if Wilt were home free. During his first six years in the National Basketball Association, Wilt Chamberlain's teams had never won anything from the Boston Celtics. And during his first six years in the NBA, Wilt Chamberlain had never received the recognition he felt he deserved. Everyone in the league agreed that, physically, Chamberlain was the greatest player in the game, the greatest ever to play the game. But, Wilt's critics pointed out, he had never utilized his all-round skills, never been the complete ballplayer he should be.

However, last season Wilt Chamberlain did just that. He started coming out to block up the middle on defense like Bill Russell of Boston. He started blocking shots like Russell. He started passing the ball, giving up shots himself to set up a teammate and get into good rebound position. And suddenly Wilt Chamberlain's team won something from the Boston Celtics. The Russell-led Celtics had won nine successive Eastern Division titles until this past season. But the Chamberlain-led Philadelphia 76ers finished a game ahead of Boston in regular-season play in '65–66.

The 76ers beat the Celtics in six of ten games, and Chamberlain did not play in one of the losses. They won every game in which Wilt out-rebounded Russell. Overall, in their head-to-head meetings, Chamberlain averaged 30.6 rebounds and 28.3 points per game to Russell's 21.2 rebounds and 9.6 points.

Between the season's close and the start of the playoffs, the league players voted Chamberlain Most-Valuable-Player-of-the-Year, and they voted 76er coach Dolph Schayes Coach-of-the-Year. Both Dolph and Wilt appeared to be extremely happy, Chamberlain particularly since he'd finally gotten recognition from his fellow players. In the past Bill Russell had won the MVP award almost as a matter of course annually. That was because Russell was the key man on a team that always won.

But now Chamberlain had won, and his team was heavily favored to win the playoffs, too. Boston, an aging team that had had many injuries, was having a hard time getting by the Cincinnati Royals in the Division semi-finals while the 76ers were relaxing.

Boston got by, though, and a funny thing happened to the 76ers on their way to an NBA championship. They were destroyed by Boston.

No one could really blame Wilt Chamberlain, who was tremendous in the Eastern finals. The only thing that he could be faulted on was his foul shooting, and at this point no one really expects Wilt to hit fouls. He simply has no touch for them and never will have.

Nevertheless, Schayes figured it wouldn't hurt for Wilt to keep trying to improve on them. The 76er coach called a team practice during the playoffs, and Chamberlain did not show up. A few days later, in the game in which Boston eliminated Philadelphia, Wilt missed 17 of 25 foul shots. In the locker room afterwards Wilt was asked about missing practice. Joe McGinniss, the probing young reporter from the Philadelphia *Bulletin,* said, "Wilt, you missed 17 foul shots tonight; don't you think you could have used some practice on the line Monday?"

"All the practice in the world ain't gonna help me at the line," Wilt said.

"Dolph asked you to report for some foul shooting," McGinniss said.

"Yeah," Chamberlain snapped, "and I told him I didn't want to because I felt some rest would do me more good. Now you get outta here."

McGinniss said he had a right to be there—and Chamberlain lunged at him. A couple of other writers and 76er scout Vince Miller restrained the biggest man in the league. They certainly deserve some kind of award.

No doubt Chamberlain was later sorry that he blew

his cool. He was angry at losing the playoffs. He was probably also angry when he realized Schayes was going to lose his job because he couldn't handle Wilt and a couple of other 76er players who had no respect for Dolph. Schayes was too easy-going, it was said, and let Wilt and others get away with too much.

But as soon as the 76ers were out of the playoffs it was rumored Coach-of-the-Year Schayes was to be fired. Milton Gross, the digging veteran writer for the New York *Post*, asked Wilt about the rumor. "I don't see how they can possibly fire him," Chamberlain said. "If I were the owner I wouldn't. What reasons can you give? We won the Division championship. Dolph was voted the most valuable coach (sic) in the NBA, and regardless how things came out in the playoffs against Boston, it was we, the players, who lost it and not the coach. He didn't lose it."

Wilt went on to explain why he missed that practice Schayes called, saying, "I had a cold all week. My nose was running; I was coughing. I had a 102 temperature and had to get a doctor. The organization knew it; the coach knew it. They practice in the Arena, and it was 25 degrees there, no heat in the place at all, so I stayed home to rest, which would do me good.

"I'm not a prima donna like they try to make me out to be," Wilt told Gross. "And I'll tell you this: I played better basketball in this last series than ever in my whole life, more complete basketball. That Sunday game on TV that we blew the lead and lost in overtime, when I had a shot I should take, I took it. In the first half I had as many rebounds as the *whole* Boston team. I played such good defense that Havlicek had only six out of 29 shots, and Sam Jones only seven out of 25. But we blew the game. And I got rapped in the papers. I wasn't supposed to be together with the team and doing what I was supposed to do."

That was ridiculous. Chamberlain had 46 points and 34 rebounds in the final playoff game. And the only reason he shot so much was because none of the other 76ers could hit the basket. Wilt did everything he could to win. He did it all season.

Schayes was talking about the "new" Chamberlain when the season was less than a month old. "Wilt's moving well inside," Dolph said, "and when he gets the ball on the move he's effective. He's working with Hal Greer on picking and rolling situations and pitching out on the fast break. Defensively he's picking up men out front. He's challenging anybody coming through the middle."

The previous season, when Wilt had been traded to the 76ers from the Warriors, he felt the team was physically superior to the Celtics. However, Wilt himself wasn't physically fit then. He had a serious pancreatic ailment that caused him to play in considerable pain in '64–65. The 76ers lost to the Celtics during the regular season but came within a basket of upsetting Boston in the play-offs. This past season, his health restored, Chamberlain was more confident than he had ever been that his team could take Boston. This doubtlessly motivated him to cut down on his scoring, do more passing, and play more defense than in the past. His goal was to win.

Even with his new outlook Chamberlain continued to dominate the league scoring race. In February, midway through his seventh season in the NBA, Wilt passed Bob Pettit to become the all-time league scoring champion. At season's end he had set five records.

It was the seventh consecutive season in which he'd led the league.

He had the highest field-goal accuracy percentage in history during 1965–66: .540.

He extended his most-games-without-fouling-out mark to 543.

He extended his most-seasons-with-over-2,000-points record to seven.

And he extended his most-points-lifetime total to 21,486.

But in the season he opened by saying, "We've got everything that's needed to win," and "my offense is nothing; I once scored 65 points in Boston and we lost," the season that looked so promising for so long, ended in controversy and frustration.

Alex Hannum, fired at San Francisco, takes over at Philadelphia this season. He and Wilt had an excellent relationship on the West Coast, and Wilt will be back to try it again. He has to believe that controversy and frustration cannot dog him forever.

BILLY CUNNINGHAM

Whether Dolph Schayes deserved to be fired as coach of the Philadelphia 76ers or not may be questionable. But that he deserves to be applauded for his handling of Billy Cunningham last season is unquestioned. Cunningham was the second-best rookie in the National Basketball Association, and he was a key factor in Philadephia's beating out Boston for first place during the regular season. But Cunningham might just as easily have spent a frustrating year on the bench if it hadn't been for Schayes's perception.

Another pretty good basketball player named Cliff Hagan did exactly that as a rookie because he was played out of position. Hagan was a center at the University of Kentucky despite the fact that he stood only 6-4. When he came into the NBA he suffered through his rookie season trying to play guard. Not only couldn't he play in the backcourt, but also his inside talents were being wasted. When Cliff went to forward in his second season he quickly became an all-star.

Billy Cunningham, who is about an inch taller than Hagan, faced a similar problem when he joined the 76ers. He played at guard. Or tried to. "For the first few days," Billy says, "I was sure I was going to get cut."

Schayes didn't see it that way at all. "After a few games," Dolph said, "we realized that Bill would never be able to take advantage of his full potential, his driving and leaping, unless we moved him inside." Although Cunningham was having trouble doing a guard's job, dribbling, ballhandling, and feeding teammates with sharp passes, he was doing other things that impressed his teammates and his coach.

"He'd make picks, move without the ball," said Dolph, "all the things I like to see in a ballplayer. If he was

46

played though, he'd fight to free himself instead of letting up. Billy's a schoolyard player. He's pure basketball. He's loose. He can give-and-go as long as you ask him. He does everything a rookie must do to make it big. First, he thinks under pressure. Second, he's a great competitor who loves to go to the boards. And, finally, he goes all out, with or without pain, as evidenced by his play late in the season even though he was bothered by a bad back for almost a month."

"I got a big lift when I moved back to forward after Dolph dropped the backcourt experiment," Billy says. "I felt more at ease and began to feel more like a part of the team, knowing I could help more up front, not only shooting but also going to the boards."

Actually, until the 76ers traded Johnny Kerr to Baltimore for guard Wally Jones early in the exhibition season, the team couldn't afford *not* to use Cunningham in the backcourt. Larry Costello had retired at the end of the previous season, and Hal Greer and Al Bianchi were the only capable guards left. Cunningham had a good attitude about the transition and never showed any displeasure. He tried, but guard just wasn't his position. Schayes says he would have made it eventually—in three to five years—but by that time he might have become so discouraged that he would have lost his game.

He was a natural at forward. Schayes was very careful in matching up Billy with the smaller forwards he could guard on defense, and he was explosive right from the beginning. In mid-November the 76ers knocked the Celtics out of first place initially. Cunningham played 41 minutes that night and took 18 shots. He hit ten of them and six fouls for 26 points. He also grabbed 15 rebounds. "A 200 per cent effort," Schayes called his performance. "The finest game any rookie has played since I've been here."

When you recall some of the great games Luke Jackson had as a rookie only the year before, that was saying something. This past season, though, Jackson had a bad leg and was benched for some 15 games. So Cunningham became a starter and played exceptional ball. Then Jackson's leg improved, he got back into shape "and we found ourselves needing someone to give us a lift in the second quarter," Schayes said, "where we had been losing a lot of big leads. We decided to use Billy that way."

Cunningham became a sixth man in the style of Boston's John Havlicek. Billy did the job so well that soon Schayes was calling him the "best sixth man in the game." Cunningham is not, of course. Havlicek is, of course. But Cunningham was not far behind Havlicek in the ability to rush into a game on an instant's notice and blow it open.

Obviously this is not an easy job. Billy never griped about his role, but he admitted he would rather be a starter. "It's tough coming in cold," Cunningham told writer Joe McGinniss near season's end, "especially in tight spots. And you feel you have to tear up the court to stay. Early in the year I had the feeling I had to score as soon as I got in, and even later I think I felt more pressure from the bench than from the court. If you miss a couple you start thinking the next chance might be your last and you hurry your move, you worry."

Schayes didn't worry. "I can remember game after game where he came in and scored six or eight points right away," Dolph said, "just what we needed. He has tremendous freelance ability. Sure, he's the kind of player who will make mistakes—he plays a loose, wide-open game—but he ventures, he gets things stirred up. And his knowledge of the game is very unusual for a rookie. He can play any system. He has good court presence."

Opponents felt Cunningham's presence, particularly during the last few weeks of the season. The 76ers were driving for the title, and again and again the lefthanded rookie out of Brooklyn and the University of North Carolina was a key driver. Against the Hawks he scored 15 points in five minutes and 19 seconds. Against the Knicks he scored 11 points in 19 minutes, including two crucial last-minute jumpers. Against the Knicks again he scored 23 points in 18 minutes. Against Cincinnati he scored nine points in the first seven minutes of the fourth quarter as Philadelphia clinched at least a tie for the Eastern Division title.

Unfortunately, he couldn't sustain this in the playoffs. In fact, Cunningham and the rest of the 76ers with the exception of Wilt Chamberlain could do nothing right in the post-season series with Boston. But Cunningham will forget that dreadful series and start again this season, hopeful of becoming a starter.

"I hope I don't stay a sixth man for long," he said last spring.

He had always been a starter in the past, the star of his team. At Erasmus High School in Brooklyn he had been good enough to draw scores of scholarship offers to college. But they were all wasting their time, because Frank McGuire had Billy locked up for North Carolina. "He was one kid I didn't have to recruit," Frank said. McGuire's sister had lived just around the corner from the Cunninghams since Billy was a child, and Frank was a friend of the family. Although Billy averaged 35 points a game for an unbeaten Erasmus team his senior year, North Carolina was the only school he visited.

During Billy's first year at North Carolina, Frank McGuire abruptly resigned. But Billy, who'd had classroom problems that freshman year, returned to school despite McGuire's absence. Cunningham became known as "The Kangaroo Kid," as a result of his jumping. Eventually, he also became an All-America and a No. 1 draft choice of the pros. He averaged 25 points a game through three years of varsity competition, but some people were not satisfied. They said Cunningham loafed at times. Others said this was just not so. How could he do less than hustle when he did everything for the Tarheels? He scored, he rebounded, he brought the ball up court . . . he did everything he could to lift a mediocre team.

The Phillips Oilers of the Industrial League made Cunningham a very attractive offer, but the 76er money looked better to a youngster who wanted to try the NBA. "I got what I wanted," Billy said, "everything I could expect."

He also got a lecture from Frank McGuire, who, ironically, had left North Carolina to coach the old Philadelphia Warriors for a year before returning to college coaching at South Carolina. "I coached the pros," McGuire told Billy, "and I know what it takes to make it. One thing they'll never forgive you for is not hustling. The day you show signs of not trying you should just pack your bags and go home."

"He hustled right from the start," said 76er trainer Al Domenico. "He was the hardest-working rookie in camp."

It paid off for Billy Cunningham—that and Dolph Schayes's perception.

DAVE DeBUSSCHERE

On September 9, 1965, Dave DeBusschere made an announcement that he may have many second thoughts about in years to come. He announced that he would no longer perform in two professional sports; he was quitting baseball. He had been pitching for the Indianapolis, Indians, a Chicago White Sox farm team, in the Pacific Coast League, and his 15-12 record was good considering the quality of the club. But when the White Sox called him up to the majors just before the Detroit Piston training camp opened, Dave said, "I'm not going to report to the White Sox. I'm going to quit baseball and concentrate on basketball. I enjoyed playing baseball, but it was inevitable that at some time I'd have to make this decision. I decided that it would be the proper time to quit now so I could be there for the opening of basketball camp."

Early in the previous season, 24-year-old Dave De-Busschere had become the youngest coach in the history of the National Basketball Association. He had been named "interim" coach to replace Charley Wolf as head of the Pistons. But during the summer of '65, Piston owner Fred Zollner had named DeBusschere as his permanent coach, and Dave felt it was time to make the break from baseball.

The White Sox, who had given DeBusschere a $70,000 bonus to sign with them, were not happy. Manager Al Lopez said, "I'm sorry to see Dave quit because I thought he had a chance to make it. But I can't blame him for choosing basketball because he was in the majors there and in the minors in baseball."

DeBusschere told us the same thing a few weeks later. "I like baseball very much," he said, "but I felt my area of responsibility with the Pistons as a player and a coach was much greater. If I were established as a major-league

51

pitcher it'd be different, but I think right now I've established myself more in basketball."

Most people feel that DeBusschere would have already made it in the majors with almost any team except the pitching-rich White Sox. Even so, though, there was no question at all about his ability on a pro basketball court. Rival coaches around the NBA regard him as one of the most valuable forwards in the league. Although only 6-6, Dave is a powerful 225-pounder who is quick, hard-nosed, and does everything pretty well. He led the Pistons in rebounding in '64 with 874 and led again in '65 with 916. He also averaged over 16 pounds per game in each season. And he could score more if he didn't pass off to teammates so much. An excellent feeder, Dave led the Pistons in assists in '64 and was second in this category in '65. He is a first-rate, all-round ballplayer.

But his team was the worst in the league. And not only that, it was the most snake-bitten team in the league. Which is why Dave DeBusschere must have had some second thoughts as early as last season about quitting basketball to concentrate on basketball. In fact, even before the season started the Pistons had been hit with enough catastrophes to boggle the mind of any coach.

First, the Pistons' leading scorer, guard Terry Dischinger, was called into the Army for two years. Then Detroit's only center, seven-foot Reggie Harding, got into trouble with police over a simple parking ticket. He had a record of several previous arrests and there was a sidewalk scuffle, for which Harding apologized. But less than 48 hours later Harding was arrested in an after-hours joint. This is a place basketball players aren't supposed to be in at any time, and especially not at 4:30 on the morning they are to take a physical at 10:30.

"I like Reggie," Dave said, "I really do. He's a very coachable ballplayer. He always did what I told him to do. But now I'm finished with him. As long as I coach the Pistons, Reggie Harding will never play another game for this team. I mean, this is ridiculous. Just after he gives us his apology, he is caught in a 'blind pig.' Listen, I don't want to play warden. If my guys want to have a little fun, okay. I like a few beers myself; I like a little fun. But you've also got to realize where your responsibilities are.

What must young people think when they read all this stuff about Reggie?"

The Pistons suspended Harding indefinitely and requested that the NBA ban him from the league. It was a strong stand for Dave DeBusschere to take. He was desperate for a center. But he was more concerned about his team's image and that of the league than he was about winning.

But that wasn't the end of the Piston catastrophes, as two minor ones and a major tragedy followed. No. 1 draft choice Bill Buntin was a long holdout, and No. 2 draft choice Tom Van Arsdale walked out of camp. Van Arsdale worked out his personal problems a day or so later and returned. The tragedy followed before Buntin came to camp—Detroit's executive manager, Don Wattrick, died suddenly of a heart attack.

So DeBusschere tried to talk to Buntin, who wanted more money to sign than he appeared to be worth. "He's being unreasonable," Dave said. "It's all right for a guy to try to get as much as he can, but he's being a little ridiculous. And nobody can even talk to him. He's got this lawyer—a sharp guy—and he does all the talking for Bill. If you ask Bill, 'How are you feeling?', his lawyer will say, 'Bill is feeling fine.' "

Actually, Buntin had by no means been a super ballplayer at Michigan. He was simply a good college player, who at 6-7 appeared much too short to play center in the pros. But he certainly had the girth when he reported. "He's way overweight," Dave said. "His big problem is getting up and down the court."

So the Pistons went into the season without an experienced center. DeBusschere, an eternal optimist, was not dismayed. "I just set my sights on making the playoffs," he said. "I think we're gonna surprise some people. I've just never seen anything like this bad luck we've had. So many things hitting a club at a certain time like we've been hit over the past few months . . . Still and all," he said with a mirthless chuckle, "you can't give up."

DeBusschere didn't. He played every game tough and remained, as former Philadelphia coach Dolph Schayes had said the previous season, "the best offensive rebounding coach in the league."

Dave DeBusschere has always been a tough competitor. A native of Detroit, Michigan, he began starring in basketball and baseball at Austin High School. As a senior, he led Austin to the Catholic League basketball championship and then on to the city championship. Finally DeBusschere led Austin to the state championship, the team finishing with a 23-0 record.

"When I graduated," he said a couple of years ago, "I guess I had about forty college scholarship offers." However, Dave didn't want to go far from Detroit. His final decision came down between Michigan, Michigan State, Notre Dame, and the University of Detroit. What could possibly be closer to Detroit than at the University of Detroit?

That's where he went. And during his years there, Detroit had its greatest basketball success ever. In three varsity seasons DeBusschere scored 1,985 points, averaging over 24 points per game. In addition he grabbed 1,500 rebounds. Dave's performance carried an otherwise undistinguished Detroit team into either the NIT or NCAA post-season tournaments for three years.

Naturally Dave pitched baseball, too. Pitched well enough, in fact, to lead Detroit into two NCAA tournaments.

He was the finest athlete in the small school's history. The University noted this fact when Dave graduated, and named a room in Shiple Hall The Dave DeBusschere Lounge. This kind of tribute normally is only given to alumni who make large financial contributions to the university. DeBusschere's contributions in athletics were regarded as equally large.

Nevertheless, DeBusschere was more highly regarded as a baseball pitcher than as a basketball player when he graduated with his degree in marketing in the spring of 1962. The White Sox and a dozen other teams all tried to sign him. Again Dave didn't want to leave Detroit and was most interested in signing with the Tigers. They refused to give him permission to play pro basketball, too, so he signed with Chicago.

DeBusschere had a pretty good rookie season, but he was downright sensational in the playoffs, averaging 20 points a game and even playing backcourt when coach Dick McGuire asked him to. He reported over a month late to spring training because of his participation in the playoffs, and teammates ribbed him about his "ghost white" appearance. They, of course, all had tans.

Al Lopez wasn't overjoyed by DeBusschere's playoff play. He said, "I know he's a fighter, and I know he can be a good pitcher. But the way he developed in basketball doesn't mean anything down here. In fact, I wish he had done real bad. Then they would have fired him."

But Dave DeBusschere did real well in basketball . . . and then fired himself from baseball.

JOHN HAVLICEK

John Havlicek is consistent in everything he does on a basketball court. He hustles consistently. He plays tough defense consistently. He scores consistently. Although he seldom starts a game, he is consistently among the Boston Celtics' top two scorers at game's end.

In the last playoff series against the Los Angeles Lakers —the one Boston wasn't even expected to be in, and, once in the finals, wasn't expected to win—John Havlicek ended up as the Celtic high scorer. You can't be any more consistent than he was in the first three games. Havlicek scored 21 points in each, and Boston had two victories. In the fourth game Havlicek went wild, as he does periodically, hitting 14 field goals and four fouls for 32 points. In the fifth game he went back to "normal," scoring 23 points, then got 27 in the sixth game. The Celtic plan in the seventh and final game was to overemphasize their defense. They did just that, winning the game and the National Basketball Association championship by the very low score of 95-93. Havlicek got 16 points in that one.

Ironically, Havlicek is not a really great ouside shooter, certainly not the kind of guy you would expect to shoot as often as he does. When he came into the NBA, after playing under the very large shadow of Jerry Lucas at Ohio State, Havlicek didn't shoot nearly enough. Lucas had, of course, done the shooting in college. Thus when John reported to the Celtics he didn't shoot, and coach Red Auerbach kept screaming at him: "Don't let them insult you [by falling off on defense]. Take your shots even when you're missing."

Gradually Havlicek began to shoot a bit more, averaging over 14 points a game his first season and being named Rookie-of-the-Year on his all-round play. In his three

NBA seasons since then, Havlicek has averaged about 19 points a game. His field-goal shooting percentage has never been higher than 42 per cent and was just under 40 per cent last season. Yet this undistinguished figure bothers Auerbach not at all. "John comes off the bench," Red says through a smile, "and he shoots, shoots, shoots."

Havlicek's rapid-fire style does bother opponents because (1) it often beats them out of ballgames, and (2) it is diametrically opposed to standard operating procedure in the NBA. On every team but the Celtics, the idea is to play for the "good" shot. Guys who fire away at the basket without, say, waiting for teammates to get into rebound position often end up in the Eastern League.

One NBA opponent of Havlicek said last season: "He'll be going down the floor on a fast break and if the defense is back, he stops and fires a 30-foot jump shot." The opposing player shook his head in disbelief.

Actually, Red Auerbach's teams have always played it this way. Larry Costello, the former Syracuse and Philadelphia guard, commented a half dozen years ago: "Auerbach tells them when they get a shot, shoot it. There's no hesitation. They don't even worry about waiting for a rebounder to get in position under the boards." Costello obviously disapproved of this break with tradition, but he did not disapprove of the results Auerbach and the Celtics got from it.

"When you see the basket," Auerbach explains, "it's like in the old days—'when you see the whites of their eyes . . . fire.' If you feel in your mind it's a good shot, take it. Basketball is a game of touch, and as long as it's a game of touch a lot of things can happen."

What can happen is that a player like John Havlicek can take 42 shots in a ballgame. No Celtic player had ever done that before, and the Celtics have had their share of rapid-fire artists, from Havlicek and Sam Jones of the present team to Tom (Tommygun) Heinsohn and Bill Sharman of the past. Havlicek's feat occurred against the Cincinnati Royals. He played only 37 minutes that night, taking better than a shot a minute and scoring better than a point a minute. He wound up with 38 points, 30 of them coming on field goals.

"One of the biggest faults I had when I came in the

pros," Havlicek says, "was my tendency not to shoot. I was looking for chances to pass, to start a play. But that changed—fast. Auerbach kept insisting I shoot."

Obviously John is not the kind of guy who refuses to follow orders. Bill Russell was another one who kept after Havlicek to shoot more as a rookie. "Russell says he would rather have *me* take the shot than *him* take the shot," John says. "K. C. Jones would rather let me shoot. But if Sam Jones is in the game, I'd rather give him the ball."

But shooting is only part of Havlicek's game. There are other reasons why John is now the best sixth man in pro basketball. Many people claim Havlicek is the best ever, though some oldtimers point to former Celtic Frank Ramsey as the best ever. Auerbach will not rate one over the other, saying, "They're different types. Both are swing men [playing in the frontcourt and backcourt] and so on, but Ramsey was a smart, scheming sort of ballplayer, and Havlicek is a better shooter, a better defensive man. The success of a Havlicek or a Ramsey is partly dependent on having a great center. Otherwise you might not gamble on the height you're giving away."

Playing forward, Havlicek often has to guard much taller, stronger opponents. Playing guard, he often has to guard much shorter, quicker and faster opponents. John says he prefers to guard the taller backcourt stars such as Oscar Robertson and Jerry West than the lightning-fast little guys such as Johnny Egan. "You don't try to stop the guys like Robertson and West," John says, "you just try to wear them out." As for playing the big forwards, that's easy on the Celtics, John says. Bill Russell covers anything that gets by you, and he also grabs almost all of the rebounds. "All I have to do against a forward," he says, "is block him out. I'm not too interested in getting the rebound, because if I block out, Bill Russell will get it. In college I'd block out and go for the rebound, too. When you're playing guard, though, defense is tougher. Guards are much quicker and have more room to maneuver, and most of the picks are coming up behind you."

Havlicek had never played guard until he became a Celtic. It was not an easy transition for him because he is not a natural ballhandler. Seeing five other guys start each game has not been easy for him either. He was always a starter himself in high school and in college. Actually, in high school in Bridgeport, Ohio, he was a starter in basketball, baseball, and football. A quarterback, he was good enough to make all-state and to be offered 35 football scholarships, including one to Ohio State. But after high school, basketball was more to his liking. It was football coach Woody Hayes, seeing he wasn't going to get John for his team, who suggested he come to Ohio State anyway and play basketball. Hayes didn't want to see an athlete of Havlicek's ability go someplace else.

John had been considering playing basketball at Ohio State all along. He became convinced that was the place to go after he'd participated in a series of high-school all-star games on the same team with Jerry Lucas. Lucas had already decided to go to Ohio State and John figured any team Jerry played for was going to be a winner.

Ohio State had quite a team with Lucas, Havlicek, and another Celtic, Larry Siegfried, on it. Lucas, naturally, was the big star and got all the publicity, but this didn't bother Havlicek. He knew that's what would happen when he decided to go to Ohio State. Probably it was because Lucas so dominated the team that the pro scouts all but overlooked Havlicek. Even Auerbach didn't know what he was getting when he drafted John. The thing is, when you win every year you get last choice in the draft and are thankful to get a solid ballplayer every few years.

"When you have last choice, you're not particular," Auerbach says. He admits he scouted Havlicek twice and "he didn't look especially good." Why then did he choose him? Red himself doesn't really know, saying, "He was a hard-nosed kid, he was well-coached, he had good fundamentals. . . ." But in the end it was essentially luck that led Red to pick Havlicek.

Very good luck, indeed, for the Boston Celtics. Very bad luck, we might add, for the Cleveland Browns, who had drafted Havlicek for the NFL despite the fact that he hadn't played college football. John just missed making the team as a receiver. In fact, the Browns wanted to keep him on their taxi squad, figuring he'd develop there and be activated to the regular squad later in the season or make the team the following year. But John had the basketball offer, joined the Celtics, and has been a star ever since. Which is consistent with his background.

BAILEY HOWELL

Bailey Howell is a garbageman. He is probably the greatest garbageman in the National Basketball Association. Now, an NBA garbageman is not a dealer in used food. An NBA garbageman deals in used shots, grabbing off all the balls under the basket that others have tried to put into the basket. Under the offensive board Bailey either rebounds his own teammate's shot and passes the ball back out, or he taps it up or shoots it up himself. Scoring on this type of close-in play is known around the league as garbage.

"I make it a point on offense," says Howell, a 6-7, 210-pound cornerman for the Baltimore Bullets, "to always go to the backboard. That means I follow every shot, whether I take it or a teammate takes it. Anyone who does that is bound to pick up a few loose balls and be able to toss them back up."

Jerry Lucas of the Cincinnati Royals may be the only forward in the league who gets better position under the basket than Bailey Howell. Bailey is not fast and he is not a great leaper like his teammate, Gus Johnson. In fact, Bailey barely manages to get his 210 pounds off the floor. But he doesn't have to because he makes sure he has position on the man he is guarding, keeping him away from the boards while watching the flight of the ball, and poising to grab it.

Actually, most fans have no idea what Howell is doing. To them he seems to be doing very little on the court. He is seldom one of the first men down on a fast break. He does not arch many 15- to 20-foot jump shots like the other forwards around the league. When he does shoot from outside—which of course he has to a few times each game to keep his defender from falling off him to help guard somebody else—Bailey's is a flat-trajectory shot. It isn't pretty, perhaps, and it doesn't capture the attention of spectators, but it is effective. And even more effective is Bailey Howell's actions after the shot. He races to the basket for the follow-up and usually manages to get a hand on the ball if the shot was off.

"I work for my points," says Bailey. "I scramble around underneath the basket, and a lot of my shots are short ones. But believe me, they are the hardest points in the world to get."

When you realize that he battles man-to-man with such powerful forwards as Lucas, Elgin Baylor, Luke Jackson, Willis Reed, and Dave DeBusschere, among others, you have some idea how hard those points are to get. Then, of course, Wilt Chamberlain, Bill Russell, Walt Bellamy, Nate Thurmond, and all the other big centers are usually under the basket, too. This is the no-man's land of professional basketball, where elbows, knees, forearms, and shoulders lash, slash, and collide. When Howell goes up for a shot underneath, usually he takes up an elbow in his side, a forearm in his neck, or a hand in his face. As he says, he pays dearly for his points.

Howell has to play this kind of hustling, all-out game because he is not a great shooter, or jumper, or speedster. Bob Pettit did all right playing the same kind of game, though he had a little better outside shot. But if others with great natural physical equipment, such as Bailey's teammate, Gus Johnson, went to the basket as consistently as Howell does, there is no telling how good they would be.

It is not a simple thing to teach. It takes discipline, determination, desire, and guts. Howell has demonstrated his guts for seven years in the NBA, and played many times with injuries that would have sidelined most players. And despite the fact that Bailey's style of play is not crowd pleasing, it pleases team officials very much. A Bullet official said when Pettit retired: "With Bob Pettit gone, Howell is the guttiest forward in the league. The average fan watches him play a game and hardly knows he's in it because they don't think he's doing anything. But you look at the statistics after the game and you see, night after night, that Bailey's scored about 20 points and grabbed about ten rebounds. He's consistent—a crucial asset to your ballclub. He does it all by going to the boards."

How did Bailey acquire this maneuver?

"Practically every coach I've ever played for emphasized this," Howell says. "At college it was James McCarthy, and during my first years in the NBA I played under Red Rocha and then Dick McGuire at Detroit. Earl Lloyd was playing with the Pistons then and he believed strongly in this part of the game. He pointed out to me how many fine ballplayers—men such as Bob Pettit and Elgin Baylor—always moved into the basket. So I made it a part of my game.

"The shots look simple, and in a way they are. But you have to follow every time, whether you are 40 points ahead or 40 points behind. You have to do it then so that when it really counts, you will automatically move underneath."

As a result of his rugged play under the boards and his hustling style of defense, Howell annually is among the league leaders in personal fouls committed. During the 1964–65 season he led the NBA in this dubious statistic with 345, cutting his total to 306 last year. Which is why Howell is among the league's leading harassers of referees. This was another trick he learned during his rookie season from Earl Lloyd and another veteran forward, Ed Conlin. "They taught me a lot," Bailey says, "how to play different guys and what to look for. But I was really surprised at the amount of complaining to the officials I saw in my first exhibition game. I asked Lloyd what was going on and he said to me: 'The squeaking wheel gets the most grease.'" The more you yell, in other words, the more officials will let you get away with. Red Auerbach could have told him the same thing.

Howell was born in Middleton, Tennessee, just nine miles north of the Mississippi border. The high school was too small to support a football team, and young Bailey found himself with nothing to do except play basketball. So that's all he did. Naturally, he became very good at it. "In Middleton," he once recalled, "basketball is just about a year-round game. Our season starts in October and we play until March, and then we keep on scrimmaging and shooting baskets until the real hot months. I started playing 'pickup' basketball in the fifth grade, and

I started playing on the high-school team in the seventh grade. I played five years and was a regular by the time I was a sophomore."

When he graduated, Bailey was sought by James (Babe) McCarthy for Mississippi State. Howell and his family liked Babe, and Bailey accepted his scholarship offer. Then he proceeded to break almost every basketball record at State and brought the school into national prominence. During Howell's junior year McCarthy said, "I'm over-board on this boy. I talk too much about him, but I guess that's because he's the greatest kid I ever saw. Just watching Howell play one time is enough to convince anybody of that. There may be other players who can do a thing or two better than he can, but I don't think there's another man in college basketball who is the all-round performer he is."

That Howell is a team ballplayer first and foremost was illustrated when as a junior he was contending for the national scoring title. State was playing Alabama and the Crimson Tide came out in a 1-3-1 zone to stop Howell. So McCarthy had his team hold the ball and wait for a good shot. At the half State led 16-8, and Bailey had four points. McCarthy went to Bailey and told him he hated to play it this way because Howell wouldn't possibly be able to score much, but it was the only way to beat Alabama. "We've got to play it this way if we want to win," McCarthy said.

"That's okay, coach," Bailey said. "Let's play it your way."

Howell was drafted by the Pistons and became a star in his rookie season. He averaged 17.3 points per game. During his next four seasons in Detroit he averaged over 21 points per game and grabbed more than 1,100 rebounds one year. He was traded to a higher-scoring team, the Bullets, before the '64–65 season, and his average fell to 19.2 points per game. But his field-goal percentage was an excellent .495. This past season Howell's average fell further, to 17.3 points per game, but it didn't bother him.

"I have no complaints," he said. "It just shows that we have more shooters on the club than we did last year, and that the Bullets are a strong ball club. I'm just glad I can do my job and contribute to a victory."

The 29-year-old Howell, an insurance salesman in the

Lew Alcindor, UCLA
(Photo: UPI)

Elgin Baylor, Los Angeles Lakers

Dick Barnett, New York Knicks
(Photo: UPI)

Rick Barry,
San Francisco Warriors
(Photo: UPI)

Walt Bellamy, New York Knicks

Bill Cunningham,
Philadelphia 76ers
(Photo: UPI)

Dave DeBusschere,
Detroit Pistons

Wilt Chamberlain, Philadelphia 76ers

John Havlicek, Boston Celtics

Bailey Howell,
Baltimore Bullets

Lucious Jackson,
Philadelphia 76ers

Jerry Lucas,
Cincinnati Royals

Gus (Honeycomb) Johnson,
Baltimore Bullets

Don Ohl, Baltimore Bullets

Willis Reed, New York Knicks

Guy Rodgers,
San Francisco Warriors

Oscar Robertson,
Cincinnati Royals

Bill Russell,
Boston Celtics
(Photo: UPI)

Cazzie Russell, University of Michigan
(Photo: UPI)

Satch Sanders,
Boston Celtics

Jerry West,
Los Angeles Lakers

Nate Thurmond, San Francisco Warriors

PRINTED IN U.S.A.

off-season, would be interested in a college coaching job when he retires in a few more years. "I'd probably teach my forwards and centers to play the same way I do," he says. "If you can get them to move into the board all the time, then you keep the pressure on the other team."

And develop more garbagemen, NBA-style.

LUKE JACKSON

Late in his rookie season in the NBA, Lucius Jackson of little Pan American College in Texas said, "This has been the biggest, most exciting year of my life . . . being drafted on the first round . . . making the Olympic team . . . the trip to Tokyo, and playing and winning a gold medal. . . . And it keeps coming. Making the 76ers . . . playing against Russell, Chamberlain, Pettit, Oscar Robertson, Jerry Lucas . . . then playing in the All-Star game. Now we've got Wilt on our side. Man, we might win the whole thing now. That would top everything."

The Philadelphia 76ers did not win the NBA championship in 1964–65. They did not even win in the Eastern Division, losing to the Boston Celtics by a single point. That frustrating defeat was a kind of prelude to Luke— as he is called by teammates—Jackson's second year in professional basketball. Although there is no question that the 6-9, 230-pound Jackson is an NBA star and quite possibly a coming superstar, his sophomore season with the 76ers was one he'd like to forget. He won't. Not for a long time.

After battling Willis Reed of the New York Knickerbockers to a virtual tie for Rookie-of-the-Year honors, Big Luke devoted his off-season to getting married and eating. He married his longtime sweetheart, Marva Prescott, and took a fancy to her fancy cooking. It was understandable that Luke wanted to rebuild his strength. He had weighed almost 240 pounds when he returned from the Olympics. By the end of the NBA season he was worn down to a bony 220. That's because he plays the game so relentlessly, never letting up. He is one of the hardest-working forwards in the league.

But when he returned to Philadelphia from his honeymoon last August, some people wondered if he wasn't working too hard at building himself up. He weighed 260 pounds. "Marriage," he said, "is really agreeing with me. I'm looking good, the picture of health. I look like Hercules." Jackson claimed his waist was the same 34 inches it had been the previous season and that he was looking forward to increasing his 15-point rookie average.

He had played half his first season at center, until Wilt Chamberlain was acquired in trade. Then Luke switched to the corner, a position he had never played before. "I learned a lot of things that shouldn't happen to me this year," he said. "My defense from the corner wasn't that good. This year I'll start at forward, and I'll be doing the things I have to do day in and day out."

However, when the exhibition season started he found the extra weight he had put on was a disastrous mistake. As happens to many overweight basketball players, he came down with shin splints. Legs pounding up and down a court can only bear so much weight. Luke realized after pounding up and down a few days that he'd never be able to play at 260, or even at 250. He pushed himself too hard too fast trying to get into condition. "I got the worst case of shin splints you can imagine," Jackson said later. "The pain burned up my legs every time I ran a step."

To make matters worse, a hamstring he had pulled late in the '64–65 season acted up. He had refused to rest the initial injury because he felt he was needed. Tape alone didn't prevent him from reinjuring the hamstring, and between seasons scar tissue had formed around it. More pain. Still Luke pushed himself as much as he could, because he has an intense desire.

But people couldn't believe he was the same player they'd seen the year before. In fact, Jackson looked so bad that his name began to pop up in trade rumors all over the league, and he played less than 20 minutes a game for several weeks.

"At first the trade rumors bothered me," Luke said in mid-November, "but now I don't pay any attention to them. I'm very happy in Philadelphia, and I'd rather play 25 minutes here than play 40 someplace else. I've made up my mind that I'm going to help the team any way that coach Dolph Schayes wants me to help. If he feels that I'm not doing the job, he should sit me down. I've just got to adjust to sitting down, and it's hard when you are used to playing all the time. Then, when he wants me to go in, I'll go in there and do my best. If my best isn't good enough, then it won't be because I didn't try."

Nobody will ever accuse Luke Jackson of not trying. Very strong and a good leaper, he is perhaps the ruggedest offensive-rebounding forward in the league. Most of his points come on driving hook shots and second-efforts because he does not have a good touch from outside. But he is a battler.

After Jackson first moved to forward, all-time St. Louis Hawks' star Bob Pettit, who was retiring at the end of that season, said, "If I'm ever tempted to make a comeback, I'll think of Jackson. You play him 10–20 minutes, it's bad enough. But he never stops on defense. If he feels you tiring, look out."

Earlier, when Jackson was still playing center, Bill Russell of the Celtics commented after Luke had outbattled him: "I have to turn the other way to breathe hard, because when he senses I'm tired he goes wild. He's good, no doubt about that—and he'll get better. You know what's good about him? When he's playing good he dominates a game. Like that stretch at the end when he made three or four hoops in a row, blocked two or three shots, and got all the rebounds. He dominated the game."

It is very difficult for anyone playing on the same team as Wilt Chamberlain to dominate the game other than Wilt Chamberlain. Nevertheless, once Luke Jackson got into shape and back into the starting lineup around mid-season, he made important contributions to the 76ers. His aggressive rebounding down the stretch, particularly, was a big factor in Philadelphia's ending Boston's long domination of the Eastern Division title. Al Domenico, the 76er trainer, did an excellent job of keeping Jackson's hamstring loose by stretching it before games and at halftime.

However, Jackson still wasn't 100 per cent physically sound. After his shin splints healed he suddenly began to have sharp pains in his right shinbone in January. At first Luke thought the splints had broken loose again. Finally X-rays were taken and initial reports had it that Jackson had been playing with a broken bone in his leg. Actually, a piece of bone had broken off.

"I don't know how it happened," Luke said, "but X-rays

showed there was a chunk of bone missing. It's not a broken leg. There's a piece of bone missing, and that's all. A bump rises there once in a while but they've told me to finish the season, and then we'll see about it."

Jackson's fierce desire is what first impressed the 76ers most. Dolph Schayes said during Luke's rookie year: "He accepts everything as a challenge. Sometimes I set a goal for him before a game, not directly but as part of our pre-game talk. Like: 'Luke will grab 20 rebounds.' And you can bet he'll battle like all get-out to grab every rebound."

When Ike Richman, the late owner of the 76ers, saw Jackson play against the Russian national team he gushed afterwards: "I think this kid is going to make us the championship team. I think we're going all the way with him. In the last game against the Russians there was no question he was the outstanding player on the floor. I think in Jackson we got the greatest. He's got Russell's timing, and he's got a great shot and he's tough. He took that 7-2 Russian and made him look like nothing. Nobody's gonna push Jackson around."

Luke did a fine job at center for Philadelphia, but when Richman had a chance to get Chamberlain he took it. Wilt, of course, pushed Jackson from center to forward. Many people thought Luke should be a little bitter about this. No doubt he regretted the switch from a personal point of view, but he realized the team was better off, and he felt no bitterness.

When the deal was made, even some NBA veterans thought it was bad and that Jackson had a right to be upset. Tom Gola of the Knicks, who played several years with Chamberlain, said Wilt would hurt the team because Jackson's skills would be wasted.

Said Luke: "Gola shouldn't have said that. I'm scoring more now with Wilt. It took me a few games to get the feel of playing forward because I played pivot all my life until Wilt came. But, heck, Wilt is the best player who ever lived and you'd be crazy if you didn't get him if you could."

The transition to forward proved difficult. Willis Reed, who Jackson admits is a better shooter than he, had sim-ilar problems adjusting to the switch this past season when

New York acquired Walt Bellamy. But Jackson finished strong and is confident he won't have any problems from now on. One thing he'll never do again is spend his off-season at a dinner table.

GUS JOHNSON

Bob Ferry, one of the NBA's great humorists and most perceptive ballplayers, was talking about his Baltimore Bullet teammate Gus Johnson last season. "If you watched Gus get dressed," Ferry said, "you'd have to applaud."

That's about as perceptive an assessment of Gus Johnson anyone could make. Gus is a spectacular fellow on and off the basketball court. He wears $200 suits, $50 shoes, $20 shirts, and a gold star imbedded upside down in an upper front tooth. "That," says Gus through a glittering smile, "is for my personality."

Johnson has always been proud of his colorful image. When he was playing high-school ball in his hometown of Akron, Ohio, Gus had a gold gypsy earring installed in one lobe. He also grew a goatee, pre-dating Bill Russell, Wilt Chamberlain, and the giant professional football tackle, Ernie Ladd, by some years.

But Gus Johnson is most colorful on a basketball court, playing the game as only he can. Johnson stands 6-5¾ and weighs 242 pounds. He is fantastically strong, second only in a league full of powerful individuals to Wilt Chamberlain, according to the men who face both of them. And Gus has the young Elgin Baylor's ability to jump off the floor and stay up in the air for what seems like a half minute at a time. All the while he's suspended, Johnson—like Baylor—can execute several twisting, turning, shifting maneuvers with his body and with the basketball before he releases the shot: underhand, overhand, sidearm with English. . . . Gus himself has no idea how many different shots he has because almost every game he seems to come up with a new one. How he releases the ball depends on how the defensive player (or players) comes at him. Then, hanging in mid-air, Gus improvises and usually manages not only to get the shot off but also to get the shot in the basket.

He is able to do one thing during his suspended maneuvers that even Baylor couldn't do in his prime. When Gus goes up he can actually leap 15 to 20 feet toward the basket before shooting. He continually amazes opponents with this ability. In a game against Cincinnati two years ago, Johnson was driving down mid-court. But just before he reached the foul line, one of the Royals loomed in front of him. So Gus leaped. Royal reserve guard Jay Arnette nudged Bud Olsen on the bench and both of them chuckled, thinking Gus had taken off too soon this time. "We're still snickering," Arnette said later, "when Johnson, still in the air, dunks the ball. None of us on the bench could believe what we'd seen."

That's because when Gus Johnson leaps he's unbelievable. You never know what he's going to do, as we said, because *he* doesn't. In a game at St. Louis the year before last, Gus drove in and went up on one of his spectacular layups, dunked the ball, and smashed the backboard. The game was held up 25 minutes while a new backboard was installed, and the players alike found time to compose themselves after the scene they'd witnessed. Johnson does that to people.

How did he develop his leaping ability? "I've always been able to jump fairly well," Gus says. "I did a little high-jumping in high school and also ran the 440 and threw the shot. Outside of that—and the fact that I had to play center in college at Idaho, often against taller men—I haven't done anything to develop my jumping ability. I've just used what I have.

"Sometimes I'm not so sure it's an asset," he adds candidly. "I have a tendency to horse around when I get up in the air. Instead of getting an easy dunk, I'll take too much time yo-yoing around and foul it up."

Why, then, does he do so much leaping? "I can't explain it— unless it's an urge to escape," says Gus, laughing. "There are so many big men in this league, I must subconsciously want to get up there where they can't bother me."

Nate Thurmond, who played ball with Johnson as a kid in Akron and then had to guard him as a cornerman with the Warriors before Wilt Chamberlain was traded, says if

Gus were a couple of inches taller nobody in the league could ever stop him. "Right now Johnson is the best all-round forward in the league," Nate says. "Bar none."

Wayne Embry, the Cincinnati Royal center, says of Johnson: "He has Elgin Baylor's equipment, only he jumps better. He's the only player I've seen go up for a rebound, take the ball at his waist, and still dunk it before he comes down on the floor."

In his first two seasons in the NBA, Johnson averaged 17.3 points and 12.2 rebounds, and 18.6 points and 13.0 rebounds, respectively, per game. This past year was supposed to be his most spectacular, the one in which he really became the superstar his skills should make him.

But Gus suffered a very serious wrist injury early in the season. Doctors said at the time that there was a definite possibility that when the broken bone healed, Gus might end up with a stiff left wrist. So they put a cast on the wrist and said a prayer. One or the other, or both, worked. When the cast came off, the wrist had its normal flexibility.

However, then Gus reinjured the wrist, back on went the cast . . . and he was sidelined for two months altogether.

"That threw my timing off," Gus said a few months after he returned to action, "and it took a while to get it back. But fortunately, I was able to stay in shape, because I could still run. The hardest part was watching the team play without me, because I think this could be a Baltimore year. We have the scorers and the depth, and by playoff time we could really be winging."

The Bullets battled the Los Angeles Lakers for first place in the Western Division all season. But they didn't begin beating the Lakers until Johnson returned. The games against LA were crucial, and Gus gave his best performances in them. He called the one March 2 in Baltimore his best of the season.

Johnson not only scored 28 points and picked off 25 rebounds, but also he passed to teammates to set up 14 more points, and he limited rugged Laker forward Rudy LaRusso to two points in the first half. Near the end, with the Bullets trailing by two points, Gus fed Don Ohl for a driving basket, then Gus hit on two free throws to put Baltimore ahead for good, and finally he intercepted a Laker pass to keep them from coming back.

"I guess that's my best over-all game this season," Gus

said in the locker room afterward. No one present that night could imagine how he could be any better.

Bullet coach Paul Seymour said the team would have had a lot better record if it hadn't been for Johnson's injury. "Gus's injury cost us eight to ten wins," Seymour said. What he meant was that instead of being 4½ games behind Los Angeles at that stage, the Bullets would have been 3½ ahead of the Lakers in first place had they had Gus all the way.

Perhaps. But the rap against Gus Johnson has always been that he is inconsistent, that he doesn't hustle one night the way he does on another. Former NBA official Charley Eckman said two years ago: "The key to this club is Gus Johnson. When he hustles, the whole team hustles—and usually wins. One night he's practically jumping up in the balcony taking tickets, and the next night he hardly gets off the floor."

Gus himself admits, "I'm inconsistent. But when my shooting is off, I try and concentrate on other parts of the game—defense, setting picks, rebounding. There's a lot more to the game than scoring."

There's a lot more to Gus Johnson than scoring, too. He can do everything you have to do on a basketball court. The Bullet management thought so much of his ability that they didn't hesitate to trade their big man, Walt Bellamy. With Bailey Howell, Bad News Barnes, Johnny Green, and Johnson, they had the best set of cornermen in the league. But the most important man was Johnson. Unfortunately, he was injured again as the season drew to a close and missed the playoffs. Without him the Bullets lost the semi-final series to a less-than-overwhelming St. Louis Hawk team that they'd handled rather easily during the regular season.

Most of the time, Gus Johnson is the most exciting player in the NBA. He still hasn't attained full superstar status because of his occasional inconsistency on the court. But in the locker room when he's getting dressed, he earns consistent applause.

JERRY LUCAS

When Jerry Lucas was about to graduate from Ohio State after three years of All-America play, he told everyone who asked about his future: "I don't want to play pro basketball. I don't want to live out of a suitcase." Besides, he went on, he felt he would be better off financially in the long run to jump right into the world of free enterprise immediately after graduation rather than after some ten years of playing pro basketball.

The Cincinnati Royals of the National Basketball Association had territorial draft rights to Lucas and offered him a three-year contract for $100,000. Sorry, Jerry said, didn't you fellas hear that I'm not playing pro ball? Then, as you'll recall, he changed his mind and decided to play pro ball. He signed a contract with a team called the Cleveland Pipers of the short-lived American Basketball League, a team hardly anybody recalls.

"Since I decided to play professionally," Lucas explained a while ago, "I decided, too, I'd play for the most money. I could make twice as much with Cleveland. Had things worked out, I'd have been much better off financially."

Things worked out so that the Cleveland Pipers and the rest of the ABL went out of business. Jerry, meanwhile, was still under contract to the Piper owners, who didn't have much money but who paid him something anyway. Just how much he has never said, but undoubtedly not as much as Cincinnati would have paid him. So in Jerry Lucas's first season as a professional basketball player he was on vacation. The following season he finally signed with the Royals. People couldn't wait to find out what he'd do on a professional basketball court.

John Havlicek, Lucas's teammate in college, had already played his first season in the NBA, and he bylined a story in *Sport* Magazine addressed to his friend. "Jerry," it began, "if you don't like living out of a suitcase . . . playing over 100 games a season . . . being away from your family for long periods . . . then being in the NBA will be tough. I'm giving it to you as I experienced it, after one season with the Boston Celtics. Every NBA rookie was a star at his college. You were rated one of the best college players in the history of the game. And I know you can become a superstar in this league because you are a fundamentally sound basketball player. You've got the speed, strength, coordination, a shooter's eye, and great defensive ability. There isn't much more anyone can have. But you have to want success 100 per cent to succeed as a pro."

Well, Havlicek and everyone else needn't have worried about Lucas on the latter count. There's nobody in the game who wants to succeed in everything he does more than Jerry Lucas. He immediately set about trying to succeed in pro basketball after a year's layoff and while switching from the center position to cornerman.

"It was a struggle," Royal coach Jack McMahon said. "I was real pleased with Lucas in training camp. He worked as hard or harder than anybody. He could have come in with the other attitude, you know."

Not really, not Jerry Lucas, who wanted to succeed. It was rough at first, but it soon got smooth for Lucas. Although he didn't shoot nearly as often as he should have, he averaged 17.7 points per game, hitting an average of almost 53 per cent of his shots. But more important, he pulled down a remarkable 1,375 rebounds. No other forward in the league came near that total, and only Wilt Chamberlain and Bill Russell among the centers topped it. In his second season Jerry's scoring average increased to 21.4 points per game. Of course, his rebounding improved, too. He grabbed 1,321 rebounds *while playing 13 less games than he had the previous year*. This past season Jerry had an unbelievable 1,668 rebounds and a scoring average of 21.5 points per game.

"He has a fantastic knack," said McMahon. "He gets to the ball at the peak of his jump. He teases you. You're about to get the ball, and he comes and plucks it right off the top of your fingers. There are guys who jump higher than he does, but nobody has better timing."

Nobody gets better rebounding position than Lucas, either. "I love rebounding," Jerry himself says. "I get paid for rebounding just as much as scoring points. Probably more so. That's why I'm so interested."

That, fans, is why Jerry Lucas is a success in everything he attempts to do on and off a basketball court. He loves basketball. He has to, playing in pain as he does from two bad knees. He missed the game when he sat out that year, even though he enjoyed being out of the limelight for that period. But he likes the money he earns at this sport, some $35,000-plus annually, and the additional income it has helped him accumulate through wise outside investments. Jerry Lucas candidly admits that he would like to become a millionaire before he is 35 years old, and basketball has helped him make a very good start on that goal.

His basketball salary may soon be the most minor source of the budding Lucas fortune, Leonard Shecter wrote last year. This is what Lucas had going for him:

● Jerry Lucas Pass-Time Games Inc., a company he owns with a partner which manufactures and sells games. It grossed $60,000 on one ingenious game, Jerry Lucas Spin-Play Basketball, in its first year and was expected to gross at least a half a million dollars in its second. And this was only a beginning for the company.

● Jerry Lucas Basketballs, which his company makes, complete with net and hoop, in four different price ranges. The longer Jerry plays, and he plans to play at least until he's 30 if his knees hold out, the more of these he'll sell. The income from this alone could provide nicely for most of us.

● Liberty American Investment Company. This is a holding company that started out owning only an insurance company which Jerry has invested heavily in and which he is a director of. Naturally, other holdings are planned for the future.

● Oil and natural gas wells. Jerry and his Pass-Time Games partner, R. Edsel Jones, have invested in eight wildcat wells. Seven of them have come in and will be paying dividends for years.

Of course, other things will come up, and Jerry Lucas will be in them. He has a tremendous amount of determination to succeed, as we said, on and off the basketball court. Most young men who want to go into business management right out of college are asked when they fill out job applications: "What would you like to do for the first 20 years?" But Jerry Lucas, as Leonard Shecter said, started at the top. Lucas set his goal, studied his investment possibilities, and went ahead and made them work. He was, for example, very impressed with a business instructor he had at Ohio State, Richard McClaine. So when he went into business, Lucas hired McClaine to help him operate his business. "I can remember when Jerry didn't have enough money to buy gasoline," McClaine said a couple of years ago. "Now he's in a good, sound business. I don't see how it can miss."

It can't, not with Jerry Lucas' desire to succeed behind it. With his knee problems, Lucas probably shouldn't even be succeeding in pro basketball, despite his many-splendored skills. But he has fought off the pain he plays in and become a superstar virtually from the moment he joined the pros. The knees were very bad his first two seasons in the league, and Jerry worked hard during the off-season to build them up. This past season they were a little better.

"They bother me off and on," Jerry said in January, 1966. "Last year I took cortisone injections. This year I'm taking anti-inflammatory pills. All summer I lifted weights with my legs, and this helped. This has been the best year for my knees in a long time. They're just beginning to hurt again, mostly after a game and when I'm in bed at night. Yes," he admitted, "the pain is awful.

"The worst time is while I'm driving a car. My legs are long [he stands 6-7] and I have to keep 'em bent. I have to stop the car, get out, and stretch when they hurt too much. But I've never missed a minute of pro ball because of my knees. I've made up my mind they'll always bother me, and I've learned to live with pain."

Lucas banged his left knee in the playoffs against Boston and was only half the ballplayer he normally is in the succeeding games as the Royals were eliminated. But the knee will be better again by next season, and only the usual pain will return. Despite that, though, and despite living out of a suitcase, Jerry Lucas will continue to play pro basketball because he loves the game he once said he'd never play.

DON OHL

Don Ohl, the most-valuable-player on the Baltimore Bullets in 1964–65 and the team's leading scorer last season, almost never came into pro basketball at all, and once he did there was a time he wished he never had. But let's start at the beginning.

Ohl, a 6-3, 190-pound guard, was an outstanding shooter at the University of Illinois. When he graduated he was drafted by the old Philadelphia Warriors, but he refused to report to them. "I wasn't sure I was good enough to play in the National Basketball Association," Don says. "Besides, I wanted to go into business." He did just that, opening an office-supplies firm and stationery store in his home town, Edwardsville, Illinois. He also signed on to play with the Peoria Caterpillars of the industrial league and led them to the national amateur championship in 1960.

He wasn't too excited about that brand of ball, though, and his business was doing well. So Don decided to quit the game entirely and concentrate on becoming an office-supplies tycoon. However, Nick Kerbawy was still general manager of the Detroit Pistons at the time. He had seen Ohl play in college and in industrial ball and thought he could become a star in the NBA. Kerbawy negotiated with the Warriors and purchased the rights to Ohl. Then he called Don and asked him how he'd like to play with the Pistons in the NBA.

"I wouldn't," said Don.

Kerbawy was persistent. He called Don again. And again. And again. "Finally," Ohl says through the wry smile he often displays, "I signed a contract just to keep him off my back. Then, in the fall, I tried out with the Pistons and my attitude changed. I found I was good enough to play in the NBA, and I realized I could keep my

79

office-supplies business going at the same time. I enjoy playing basketball, and I've been able to build my business. It has worked out wonderfully."

Except for the Big Bad Wolf period. That would be the time when Charley Wolf, who had been fired as coach of the Cincinnati Royals, was hired to coach the Pistons. Dick McGuire had been the Piston coach, but he quit, saying he wanted to return to his family in New York. McGuire did a very good job with unexceptional personnel, getting into the playoffs. The only thing Wolf got into was bad relationships with his ballplayers—with Don Ohl particularly.

Charley started off badly in training camp, which was located only 30 miles from Detroit, yet the players were not permitted to have cars. They couldn't leave the place without an okay from Wolf, and without cars they couldn't leave very well anyway. When they needed haircuts, they had to go as a group into town in a small truck. One player was appointed as a non-commissioned officer to keep track of the others and—believe it or not—report back to Wolf.

Perhaps the strict regimentarian's worst move as far as the over-all team was concerned occurred after an exhibition game in Toledo. The wives of several of the players drove down to view the game, then expected to drive their husbands back to camp. Wolf made all the players return in the team bus.

But the worst mistake Wolf made as far as Ohl's morale was concerned occurred when camp opened. "He walked up to me and told me he didn't like me," Don recalled. "This was the first or second day of training camp. No, he didn't give me any reason for saying this. I didn't know the man. I had never met him before. So it was a little bit unusual, I thought." Ohl, you'll note, has a marvelous way with understatement.

How did he react to his new coach's attitude? "I didn't know how to take it," Don said. Then he smiled. "I was flabbergasted at the time. Because he had no basis for saying that, I don't think. But I didn't ask him why he felt that way. So when the season started it was a strained situation. I'd never been in a situation like that before, so I was as confused as everyone else was."

And all of the Pistons were confused. Bob Ferry, who

was traded at season's end along with Ohl and Bailey Howell to Baltimore, says, "Charley restricted our play—mentally and psychologically. It wasn't exactly a personality clash. Charley had a lot of fine qualities. But he had the knack of handling things the wrong way."

In February Wolf suddenly benched Ohl for several games accusing Don of "lackadaisical" play. When a Detroit newspaperman got the story, it got into the papers and made the Ohl-Wolf relationship even more strained.

"Finally I began to lose my confidence," Don says. "My scoring fell off, my shooting percentage fell off—everything was below par. It set me back a year or two, and I had just come off my best season."

The previous season, 1962–63, Ohl had averaged 19.3 points per game on a field-goal percentage of .439, which is not bad for an outside shooter. (Oscar Robertson and Jerry West hit about .475 percent of their shots from the floor—but they are definitely out of sight.) Under Wolf's careful guidance Ohl's average fell to 17.3 points per game in '63–64 and his field-goal percentage to barely over .40.

"I was getting close to having my career ruined by what Charley said in the papers," Don says. "The other owners see that, and it hurts your stock in the league. I knew I'd have to be careful when I came to Baltimore because everyone would be looking for a reason or excuse to believe what he said was true. I knew I'd always tried my best."

The Bullet management obviously didn't believe Ohl was a lackadaisical ballplayer. Otherwise they wouldn't have given up high-scoring Terry Dischinger and young Rod Thorn, who was also highly regarded, to get Ohl and the others. In his first season in Baltimore, in '64–65, Don averaged 18.4 points per game and was named MVP of the Bullets. This past season Ohl led the Bullets in scoring with a 20.6-points-per-game average and lifted his field-goal percentage màrk to .445.

When he was asked last season to explain why he was scoring more, the wry Ohl replied, "That's easy—I shoot a lot."

That's true, but when he gets serious he says at least part of his success lies in the fact that he's no longer playing for Charley Wolf. "I don't feel any vengeance toward the man," Don says. "He's a gentleman. But I have to say I feel this is one of the reasons."

Another reason, he feels, is simply that he's been playing basketball so long that he should be able to score readily. "I'd like to say my scoring is due to hours of extra practice time," he says, displaying that wry smile, "but that just wouldn't be true. We play so much that practice is more of a luxury than a necessity. Besides, I've been playing this game since I was nine years old . . . and that makes me a 20-year man. A fellow who has been playing that long should be able to put the ball in the basket."

When Don first started playing basketball he was so short he had no idea he'd ever be able to make a career out of it. In fact, by the time he reached Edwardsville High School he was only 5-4. Yet he was very fast and a pretty good shooter and he became the eleventh man on the varsity even though he did have to wear a uniform that didn't match his teammates'.

Basketball is very big in southern Illinois (it actually supported the entire Edwardsville athletic program in Don's day there) and Ohl got a lot of practice. "They used to let us out of our last period, usually a study hall, to practice," Don remembers.

He developed his jump shot in high school, and now he is known as one of the fastest shooters in the NBA today. He had to get it off fast then because of his lack of height, just as he does in the NBA against bigger men. By his junior year at Edwardsville Don had grown to 6-1, and he was 6-3 by the time he entered Illinois.

When he graduated and was playing ball in Peoria he met the girl he married, Judy, and they now have two children.

Although he wasn't anxious to play in the NBA initially, Don Ohl is happy he finally decided to give it a try. Despite his bad experiences with Charley Wolf, he loves basketball . . . and the $23,000 salary the Bullets paid him last season didn't hurt his desire any, either. His biggest disappointment was in being eliminated from the playoffs last season. Both Ohl and Gus Johnson were injured. But Don has high hopes for the coming season, as long as a wolf named Charley doesn't show up in Baltimore. When coach Paul Seymour resigned last season, Don breathed a sigh of relief when the new Bullet coach turned out to be nothing more than a farmer named Mike.

WILLIS REED

The 1965-66 National Basketball Association season started very badly for Willis Reed. He had two traumatic experiences. The first did not have lasting effects on Willis's play, and he shrugged it off with the air of a man who has been through this before. Reed broke his nose in a pre-season scrimmage.

Teammate Bad News Barnes went up for a rebound with Willis, and Reed learned why Barnes is called Bad News. Barnes's elbow relocated Reed's nose on his cheek. "It looks like my nose is my biggest problem," Willis said. It was the fourth time it had been broken. The first occurred in a high-school football game when Willis was a guard. It was re-broken near the end of his senior year of playing basketball at Grambling College. It was re-re-broken in the last game of his rookie year with the New York Knickerbockers. Willis regarded that one, in St. Louis, as a good break. "The doctor out there just pushed it back into place," he said. "This time they put about 12 needles up my nose." He shuddered, then added, "I'm afraid to tell my wife what happened. Every time I get hurt it shakes her up."

Reed's next traumatic experience shook him up. The Knicks abruptly traded for center Walt Bellamy, and Willis was no longer a center. He was suddenly a center trying to play forward in the NBA. It was a shock to everyone on the team. First of all, the players had no idea that Bellamy was available. Secondly, the Knicks already had a center, one W. Reed. After over a decade of playing large people like Ron Shavlik, Gary Bergen, Art Spoelstra, Jim Palmer, Ray Felix, Charlie Tyra, Gene Conley, Phil Jordan, Darrall Imhoff, Paul Hogue, Bob Nordmann, and Tom Hoover at center, the Knick management finally seemed resigned to never coming up with a good big man.

Which is why when they had a chance to draft Willis Reed on the first round in 1964, they didn't. They chose Barnes, who seemed certain to become a superstar forward in the NBA. Fortunately for the Knicks, when it came their turn in the second round, Reed was still available, and he was chosen as kind of an afterthought. And he turned out to be a better ballplayer than Barnes. The 6-10, 235-pound Reed made the All-Star team and went on to be named NBA Rookie-of-the-Year. The Knicks finally had a good young center and seemed set at the position for years to come.

However, when they learned the Bullets were interested in trading Bellamy—generally regarded as one of the three best centers in the league—the Knicks couldn't resist. After all those years of frustration in trying to fill their pivot, who can blame them?

Well, Reed, perhaps. Only a year before, after his third game against Reed, no less an authority on centers than Bill Russell of the Celtics said, "Willis is the best center I've ever seen play for the Knicks." Similar comments were heard all around the league. Everyone liked Reed's chances of becoming one of the top three centers in the league in a few years.

As a rookie Willis scored 1,560 points, and Wilt Chamberlain and Bellamy were the only rookie centers to beat that total. Reed also pulled down 1,175 rebounds, breaking the all-time Knick record set by Harry Gallatin.

But here he was as a second-year man becoming a rookie all over again. And the switch of Reed to forward was by no means illogical when New York had the opportunity to acquire Bellamy for Barnes, Johnny Green, and Johnny Egan. Former Knick coach Joe Lapchick called Reed as a rookie "the best shooter the Knicks have had since Carl Braun." Willis had proved himself to be not only a fine scorer around the boards, but an excellent outside shooter as well. There was a memorable game his rookie year against Chamberlain when Willis tried to draw Wilt outside. He did this by taking seven successive jump shots from 15 to 20 feet out . . . and hitting seven successive jump shots. No one could remember another man his size being that accurate from that distance so consistently. A lefthander, Reed shoots a high, arching, virtually unblockable jumper.

Still, he found the shift to forward a very difficult one.

He was used to turning and shooting facing the basket, but he was not used to getting open as a forward, to moving without the ball, to passing from outside. And he had a lot of trouble guarding the quick, smaller forwards around the league. All these problems played on his mind and affected his shooting. Even though Reed made the All-Star team at forward, it wasn't until late in the season that he began to feel comfortable in his new position. His scoring fell from a 19.5 average to 15.5 points per game, and his rebounding total fell to 883. But overall, the Knicks appeared more than happy with Reed's progress. They expected him to take a little time to adjust and figure he'll be a solid forward for many years now.

Willis himself wasn't satisfied with his performance and knows he will do better. Of course, Willis has a lot of confidence from his history of battling back against big odds. When he was in high school Willis grew so fast that it affected his coordination. So he went out into his backyard, put up a basket, and practiced shooting and skipped rope until he became agile again. When he went to Grambling Willis was rated no better than a second-string center behind Tommy Bownes. But Willis drove himself in practice until he was out-playing Tommy Bownes. Reed became Grambling's starting center.

At the close of his college career Reed had two bitter disappointments. First, he was not selected to play on the U.S. Olympic team that went to Tokyo. Second, he was not a No. 1 draft choice of the pros. Then, when he joined the pros, he was rated behind Lucius Jackson of the Philadelphia 76ers in the early race for Rookie-of-the-Year honors.

Reed learned of the initial disappointment when he returned home from a day of student teaching at a high school in his hometown of Bernice, Louisiana. Eddie Donovan, general manager of the Knicks, called and asked him what he thought of playing pro basketball in New York?

"I'd like that very much, Mr. Donovan," Willis said.

"Good," Donovan said, "because we just drafted you on the second round."

"I was disappointed," Reed told writer Phil Pepe last season. "I saw $3,000 flying out the window, but it wasn't only the money. My pride was hurt. I expected to be picked on the first round, which would have meant that somebody considered me the best player in the country. I couldn't blame the Knicks. Taking Barnes was a good move, and I guess I expected it. But I couldn't believe there were eight other players in the country better than me."

Barnes had made the Olympic team and reported late to the Knicks. When he came in and got adjusted, there was no doubt that he was going to be a fine pro. But by that time there was also no doubt that Willis Reed was a better pro. The only question then was who was the best rookie in the league, Reed or Jackson of Philadelphia. At that time Willis said he was pleased that Jackson seemed to be the early favorite.

"This is what I'm willing to believe," Willis said. "I want to give him all the advantages because that will make me work harder. I don't want to be complacent. I want to be Rookie-of-the-Year more than anything. He made the Olympic team and I didn't. He was picked second, and I was picked tenth in the pro draft. I guess that means a lot of people think he's better than me, so I guess his chances of being Rookie-of-the-Year are better than mine.

"Well, I'll tell you, I've played against him and he's not better than me, and he wasn't better than me in college. I played for a Negro school, and his school was integrated, which meant he played against some of the big-name schools, and he got more publicity than I did. I know my weaknesses. I'd be a fool to say I'm as good as Oscar Robertson, but I know I'm better than Jackson."

In the ultimate voting, Reed was considered better than Jackson. He admitted afterwards that he'd worked hard for the honor. "I found not everybody was going to pat you on the back," Willis said. "Somebody is always going to tell you you can't do it, and that infuriated me. Some people belittled me and questioned my ability.

"In this game it is the survival of the fittest. The strong survive, the weak do not. Now when I play, I look at those other coaches around the league and I say to myself: 'I told you so . . . I showed you.' I'm planning to make them remember that draft for a long, long time."

Last year Willis Reed worked hard to show them he

could play forward in the NBA. This season he will work still harder to show them that he can be one of the very best forwards in the league. We wouldn't bet against his proving it, either.

OSCAR ROBERTSON

With ten games left in the last National Basketball Association season, the Cincinnati Royals felt they were in position to move out of third place. They had been third most of the season but now they were within striking distance of both Philadelphia and Boston in the Eastern Division race. The Royals were to play the 76ers, whom they'd beaten three days earlier, 102-100, and were confident they could keep beating. But Philadelphia won this game, 107-103, and kept winning. Cincinnati collapsed, losing nine of its last ten games. And Royal coach Jack McMahon said just before the playoffs: "That loss to the 76ers is what killed us. People cannot understand why our record has been so bad, but that game did it. It relegated us to third place and took all the incentive out of it for us."

The thing people couldn't understand was how a team with a ballplayer the caliber of Oscar Robertson had collapsed. More than any other professional basketball player —more than Bill Russell of Boston, more than Jerry West of Los Angeles, more than anyone else in NBA history— Oscar Robertson *controls* a ballgame. He brings the ball down the court, he sets up his teammates with pinpoint passes, and he causes opposing teams to concentrate their defenses on stopping his own incredible scoring ability. Naturally, McMahon was asked what happened to Oscar during the losing streak—had he let down, subconsciously at least, along with his teammates?

"They should all be competitors like Oscar," said McMahon.

Oscar Robertson never lets down. He has too much pride to ever let down on a basketball court. He is without question the most talented all-round player in the game. Many people feel he is the most valuable player in the game. A poll of NBA players a couple of years ago asked the question: "If you could pick any man in the league for a teammate, which player would you choose?" Bill Russell was the choice of most players, but close behind him was Oscar Robertson. Said veteran Tom Gola: "Whoever plays with Robertson in the All-Star game is the winner, every year. Every team needs the big man. You take Russell, and I take Chamberlain. Whoever takes Oscar will win. He controls the ball, brings it up by himself. He can maneuver and hit the open man." This summarized the feelings of the players who regard Robertson as the most talented player in the league. Certainly he is the best of the non-giant players, and certainly he ranks right up there with Russell and Chamberlain.

This past season Robertson was third in the league in scoring, with a 31.3 points-per-game average (behind Chamberlain's 33.5 and Jerry West's 31.4) and led the NBA in assists—as he does annually—with 847, an average of 11.1 per game. In addition, Oscar hit on .475 per cent of his shots from the floor, the most accurate mark in the league among guards, and on .842 per cent of his freethrows, ranking sixth in the NBA in that category. What's more, he grabbed 586 rebounds, an unusually high total for a backcourt man.

What made his performance all the more amazing last season was the fact that Oscar missed all of the pre-season training camp and virtually all of the exhibition season. He was a holdout. Both Bill Russell and Wilt Chamberlain received $100,000 contracts for the '65–66 season. Since Robertson is regarded by so many people as the equal of these tall superstars, he felt he should be paid approximately as much money as they get. This did not seem, to the average fan, to be unreasonable.

The only trouble is that Oscar plays for a less well-to-do ownership than do Russell and Chamberlain. The Cincinnati franchise does not have the income potential of Boston or Philadelphia, even though all the NBA teams benefited to the tune of some $75,000 apiece from a new television contract. Reportedly Oscar was already earning $75,000 a year, and the Royals were also paying another superstar, Jerry Lucas, somewhere in that high-priced neighborhood. Neither Boston nor Philadelphia have two such superstars. What it came down to, for the Royals, as general manager

Pepper Wilson said, was: "We're getting priced out of what we can handle."

Cincinnati said it couldn't pay, and Oscar said if it couldn't pay he couldn't play. But, of course, he did, signing for a token raise. He reported late and was out of shape for the season's first few weeks, but you could hardly tell it from his performance. An interesting thing happened, though, when the season ended. Knowing the problem Royal management faced—and would face again, no doubt, at contract time this year—the New York Knickerbockers tried to make a deal with Cincinnati for that fellow O. Robertson. What did they offer?

A $350,000 package, that's what.

No other player in the history of basketball had ever been sought for that kind of package. But that's what the Knicks offered in money and players, according to Leonard Lewin, the knowledgeable basketball writer for the New York *Post*. Remember, too, the Knicks have some superstars of their own to offer now.

New York is not only a more financially sound franchise, it is potentially a "sell-out" city. That is, even the last-place Knicks draw extremely well, and once they become a winning team they are expected to become virtually sold out at home. The Knicks are building toward a winning team now. But the point is, Oscar Robertson could make them winners instantly.

Robertson kept the Royals in contention for the Eastern title almost by himself for years. Now he has Jerry Lucas helping him, and now the Royals are solid threats. In the last three seasons the Celtics have won only three more games from Cincinnati than the Royals have won from Boston. Last season these two teams played evenly, Cincinnati winning four out of five at home, Boston winning four out of five at home. So, despite their late-season collapse, the Royals were confident when they went into the last playoffs against the Celtics.

They started off playing like their confidence was justified. Robertson led the Royals to two straight wins, one in Boston, and the team didn't play badly in the next game, a loss in Cincinnati. But in the following game Cincinnati had problems right away as Oscar got into early foul trouble. When Robertson picked up his fifth personal, defensive specialist K.C. Jones came back into the game to pressure and harass him. Jones, one of the closest defenders in the league, was all over Oscar as Robertson moved in toward the basket. Oscar looked around to pass, but Jones wouldn't give him an opening. So Oscar twisted to his left and hooked . . . and the Royals were back in the game. However, moments later Robertson committed his sixth foul. When he went out of the game, something went out of his teammates. Even the casual fan could see they seemed to lose heart.

That, as it turned out, was the crucial game of the play-offs. The Royals never bounced back. They appeared to have Boston down with those two opening wins, but after they lost Oscar in that game in which Boston tied the series they just didn't seem to feel they could win. There's only so much even a ballplayer like Oscar Robertson can do.

He does so much, perhaps his teammates have come to rely too heavily on Robertson. But you can see why the Royals could never afford to trade him. The management would be run out of town.

It is unfortunate that Robertson has never played on a title team in professional basketball. He has achieved everything else in the game. But he has never played on a championship team in the pros, or even in college, for that matter. The last team Oscar led to a title was Crispus Attucks High School in Indianapolis, Indiana. He led the Indians to 45 straight victories and two successive state championships.

"It was a great thrill," Oscar said a couple of years ago. "After the game, the local fire department was there with the fire truck, and we all got aboard and rode through town with the siren going. Then we had a bonfire and everything. It was sort of inspiring; it really was."

Not as inspiring as Oscar Robertson on a basketball court. He's a very intense ballplayer, a fellow who obviously wants to win more than anything. Yet winning is something that has eluded him all these years since high school. Which is one reason why last season, when the Royals were in good position twice to make that title move, their collapse was such a disappointment to Robertson. The only thing is, you have to figure a guy with all his talent just can't avoid playing with a winner one of these seasons.

GUY RODGERS

For some three weeks last season Guy Rodgers of the San Francisco Warriors went berserk. You remember Guy Rodgers, don't you, folks? Sure, he was the fellow who was known for his good passing, weak shooting during his first seven seasons in the National Basketball Association. But that was before Guy Rodgers went berserk early last season.

It all started two games before San Francisco's good-shooting guard, Paul Neumann, broke his finger playing against the Los Angeles Lakers. Rodgers had two good-shooting games in a row. And now, since the Warriors had no other outstanding shooter to send into their back-court, little Guy Rodgers decided, what the heck, he might as well throw a few balls at the backboard for a change. The funny thing was that most of them started flying through the basket. The night Neumann was injured Rodgers scored 47 points. That's right—47 points! Nobody could believe it. Guy Rodgers, who had never scored more than 33 points in an NBA game before last season, got 47 in one ball game.

That wasn't all, though. Guy followed that all-time high with 23 points, then 39, 46, 37, and 37. All told, he averaged 36 points through eight ballgames. His team-mates couldn't even believe it, and certainly Rodgers himself had no idea what was happening. It was just that somebody had to shoot from the backcourt, and once Guy got going there was no stopping him for three weeks. Pop, pop, pop. There were driving layups that he ladled up underhanded, tossed up from the side, arched up from the shoulder . . . There were jump shots that he shot from the corner, from the foul circle, from 25-feet out. . . . There were bank shots, there were tap-ins, there was every

93

conceivable shot in and out of the book; but they kept going into the net.

It reached the point where Warrior players and coach Alex Hannum were sitting on the bench talking to themselves. About Rodgers. "I thought I was beginning to see things," Hannum told magazine writer Frank Deford. "So finally, when Guy did one more fantastic thing, I turned to Gary Phillips next to me and I said, 'Gary, am I wrong? Has he ever done that before?' And Gary just shook his head and said, 'No, Alex, I'm sure he's never done that before. I've played with him and I've guarded him, and I've never seen him do that before.' And then he did something else, so we just sat there and shook our heads some more."

Opponents were shaking their heads, too. After Rodgers scored 37 points against the St. Louis Hawks, player-coach Richie Guerin said, "Those were the kind of shots we want opposing players to take. They were unbelievable shots. But they just kept going in."

Actually, Rodgers has never been as bad a shooter as some people tend to think. He had scored over 6,000 points in the NBA going into '65–66. He had averaged 11.9 points per game through seven years. During the '64–65 season he had averaged 14.6 points per game, which is not bad at all for a player who is essentially a play-maker, a playmaker so good, in fact, that he is regarded as being second only to Oscar Robertson. Rodgers actually beat out Robertson for the league leadership in assists a few years back.

Still, a 36-point average, even for only eight games, startled the world of pro basketball. What's happening? people kept asking. Guy is not the type of person who speaks easily about his own accomplishments. But he did try to explain his new-found shooting ability because people started saying, Yeah, sure, he's always been a good shooter except he's always played with Wilt Chamberlain and all he ever did was feed the big man and not shoot himself. Rodgers didn't want Wilt, his long-time friend, to be criticized.

"Certainly it wasn't as natural playing with Wilt," Guy told Deford. "We were all more like specialists. But don't make it sound like this was his fault. When Wilt Chamberlain is on your team, you have to play to him. He is just so good. But things are more flexible now with Nate [Thurmond] underneath. It is more spread out with him, and more things just seem to happen when the lane is opened up [down the middle for driving and forcing the action]. When Wilt was in there, even if they gave me the lane, when I got there, there he was and there was his man. This is more natural now. It's easier and you can do more things."

Rodgers didn't mean to criticize Wilt, but the fact remains that Guy did become a better all-round ballplayer once Wilt was traded. Guy's average went up in '64–65, and it went way up this past season. In fact, Guy was the second-leading scorer on the Warriors, averaging 18.6 points per game and 10.7 assists as well. His assists mark was just four-tenths of a point behind Robertson's. As it turned out, it was not that Rodgers shot any better than he had in the past (his fieldgoal percentage going into last season was .380, and that fell slightly to .373), but he shot more often and was more valuable. By driving more and shooting more, Guy forced the action more. Also, he forced opponents to stay with him more on defense rather than falling off on other Warrior shooters.

Of course, Rodgers has always been an extremely valuable ballplayer. "Guy is the best dribbler, the best playmaker, and the best passer in the game," Hannum said last season, "And this includes Oscar." Few people other than Rodgers's own coach would go that far, but certainly Guy is the only ballhandler in the league who compares to Oscar and has been since Bob Cousy retired. Many opponents say Rodgers is the toughest man in the league to take the ball away from. He's short, probably a bit under six-feet tall despite the program propaganda (Johnny Egan of the Bullets is slightly under 5-11 and he's listed at 6-0, too, because the NBA hates to admit a normal-sized person can play in it), and he dribbles the ball low, fast, and well. It was because of his lack of size that Rodgers developed his amazing dribbling, ballhandling, and passing skill.

Hannum has said, "Rodgers far overcomes his size handicap by being the best middle man on a fast break since Bob Cousy, and almost as great a speed-dribbler, play-starter and feeder as Cousy was. Guy can outmaneuver and upset the giants. I defy any club to try a full-court press on my team. We'll break it down every time, mostly because of Guy's ability to anticipate and his quickness in retaliating." (Hannum, of course, is now the Philadelphia coach, and he will admittedly miss Rodgers's playmaking skills since the 76ers' one lack is just such a feeder.

Never be fooled by Rodgers's lack of size, though, into thinking he'll back down from you on a basketball court. He's tough because he has to be, and NBA opponents are well aware of this at this late date. There was the game in Madison Square Garden early in Guy's career, for example, when during a battle for a ball Rodgers and Carl Braun, a tall guard for the Knicks, got into a fight. Guy took a punch at Braun and realizing he wouldn't stand a chance in a fist fight, Rodgers grabbed a stool from court's edge. "I ran over and got a stool and fought him with that," Guy said later. "Got a standoff, too."

A couple of years ago Rodgers got into an argument with Kevin Loughery and hit the bigger guard so fast he didn't need a stool. "Anyone my size can't back down for an instant," Guy says simply. "You have to string them when they string you and use your fists when strategy doesn't work. At my position, you have to apply physical contact when the other man isn't expecting it—upset him, make him worry. You have to spoil his concentration at all times on defense.

"My philosophy can be summed up this way: The regular players in the NBA and the superstars are divided by just one thing. The average player concentrates hard and plays to win. But the great ones—like Wilt, and Oscar, and Elgin Baylor—are absolutely psycho about the game. Even when they're knocked all out of shape on a drive, they never lose sight of the basket, and they make the great shot. These are possessed men."

Guy Rodgers was a possessed man for a good chunk of last season. For a change, he had the opposition upset and worried about his offensive play more than by his hawking defensive tactics. Unfortunately, Rodgers's completely freelance game had to end. Hannum felt the Warriors were getting a little too undisciplined, and he had Rodgers go back to feeding more, concentrating particularly on getting the ball into Thurmond and Rick Barry. The transition back to being primarily a feeder was not difficult at all for Rodgers. It is what he does best. He was still shooting a bit more than he had in other seasons, and finished with an 18.6 points-per-game average. But, of course, going berserk for a while had been a lot of fun for Guy Rodgers, too.

BILL RUSSELL

Funny how things work out. When Bill Russell of the Boston Celtics went in to discuss his contract for the 1965–66 season, Bill said he had decided that would be his final season. He had turned 31 the previous February, the game was becoming a grind for him, and he no longer had to play basketball for a living. His investments had made him a wealthy man.

However, Wilt Chamberlain had signed a three-year contract only a week before with the Philadelphia 76ers for a reported $100,000 per season. And when Russell went in to see Celtic coach and general manager Red Auerbach, Red asked him what he wanted.

"A dollar more than Wilt," Russell said.

So Bill, who was going to quit after one more year, signed for three more—at a salary of $100,001 per season. Not bad for a guy from a poor family in Louisiana who later moved to California and became relatively prosperous. Yet when Russell was the star of the great University of San Francisco basketball team, he once found himself without the 50-cent toll to cross a bridge to pick up a letter from President Eisenhower inviting him to the White House. Funny how things work out.

Naturally William Felton Russell was in a jovial mood when he signed what Auerbach called "an unprecedented three-year contract at a fantastic salary." Said Bill: "I called my Dad in Oakland, California, and told him I didn't want him to work any more. My Dad said, 'Listen, I'm going to keep working. I've given this company 18 good years of my life. Now I'll give them a couple of bad years.'

"It may turn out that way for me," Russell said. "If I find after three years that I am really over the hill and can't go any more, then I'll sign on for another year."

It looked like it was turning out that way for Bill much of last season. He did not play with the old verve and hustle of the Bill Russell who was almost annually the NBA players' choice as most-valuable-player in the league. At the All-Star break one rival coach was heard to say, "Wilt owns Russell now." *Newsday* columnist Stan Isaacs asked Russell about this.

"There's no doubt that Wilt's been outplaying me," Bill said with his usual frankness. "Philadelphia has beaten us three out of four games. And there's no question about how great Wilt is; he's always been great. But I don't think it's because I'm getting old. I'm as good as I ever was physically, I think.

"It's a mental problem with me. I've become sort of a fat cat. I'm not getting up for games the way I used to. Remember how I almost always vomited before a game because I was tense? Well, I hardly do that any more.

"I don't think that's so strange. When we came into the league St. Louis was great, and we got ourselves up to beat them. Then it was Los Angeles and Philadelphia and San Francisco and Cincinnati, and now there's Philadelphia again with Wilt. It's hard to keep getting yourself up all the time. But the important thing is which team wins; individuals aren't that important. And I think Cincinnati is more of a threat to us than Philadelphia. So it's more of a thing to get up for Cincinnati than Philadelphia, I would say."

The same coach who said Wilt owned Russell halfway through the '65–66 season pointedly added: "But if it came down to one game, I would have to pick Russell and the Celtics over Wilt and Philadelphia."

The coach was right on both counts. Russell didn't really play back to his old form until the last month of the season. But the biggest reason was not because of an inability to get up for games, it was because of injuries to his legs that plagued him all through the season. In fact, almost every player on the Celtics missed games and was hampered in many others as a result of injuries. Russell, K.C. Jones, John Havlicek, Sam Jones, Larry Siegfried, they all played with pulled muscles, sprained knees, twisted ankles.

But Russell's was the worst. From mid-February till the season ended with the NBA championship finale on April

28, Bill played with his entire right thigh encased in bandages and tape. "The only thing I'm unhappy about," Bill said when he found out how serious his injury was, "is that it throws my timing off. I'm disgusted about it. I'm going to have to regear and learn how to compensate. But I'll play. Listen, that's what they pay me for, right? That's why I'm supposed to be a champion, right? I'll rest the leg this summer."

Trainer Buddy LeRoux, who normally doesn't talk about injuries and seldom praises an athlete, said, "Bill's in pain. It will hurt him every move he makes. There will be times when he's really going to hurt. The only cure would be to rest, but it's not possible now. On the other hand, it's not the kind of injury which will be permanent. It will cure itself over the summer. This is one of the remarkable things about Russell. Some athletes would baby themselves. Naturally they want to protect their careers. They don't want to aggravate an injury. But Russell is intelligent. He can put his mind over a matter like this. He just faces the pain and plays with it. If it comes to a point where he can be crippled or something, he'd stop. Otherwise, he'll play."

Russell said simply: "This [basketball] is my business. How many guys go to work with a headache? So I go with a leg ache. What difference? I've been disgusted with the way I've been playing this year. I haven't had it sometimes. I guess you get older and slow up, but I'm not that old yet. I had trouble in San Francisco with Nate Thurmond [the Warrior center]. I had him good in the first half, but the leg and my stamina gave out on me in the second half, and we blew it. I paced myself a little better against LA Saturday. That's what I have to learn about now."

He must have learned about it well. The Celtics fell behind the 76ers with ten games to play and knowing they couldn't afford to lose another . . . they won each of their remaining games. The only trouble was that the 76ers kept winning, too. So for the first time in ten years the Celtics did not win the Eastern Division title. That meant they had to play in the opening round of the play-offs for the first time in a decade, against Cincinnati. The Royals won the first two games and appeared on their way to dumping Boston right out of the finals against Philadelphia. Critics said the Celtics were getting old, which was true, but the Celtics said they weren't that old, which was also true.

Boston came back to beat Cincinnati.

Then Boston easily defeated Philadelphia, despite heroic efforts by Chamberlain.

And, finally, in the championship playoffs against Los Angeles, the Celtics beat the Lakers. Funny how things work out.

For Bill Russell it was one of his greatest series. In the seventh and final game Russell, of course, led the Celtics in rebounds, grabbing 32, and he also led the Celtics in scoring, with 25 points, which is not a usual occurrence. But the most amazing part of his playoff performance was the fact that Russell played with a broken bone in his leg.

However, an even more amazing thing happened during the playoffs. Red Auerbach announced that he had finally found his coaching successor for the Celtics. And Bill Russell became the tallest coach in the league . . . and the first Negro to be elevated to so high a position in a major professional sport.

Thus it was not surprising when Russell was so emotional after the Celtics had won the NBA championship for the ninth time in the last ten years. "It was great to win it," Bill said. "Auerbach is the heart of the Celtics and it would have been a shame not to win it in his last season as coach."

Later Bill said, "We held each other's hands all season on this team. It is a family team. There were many times we were depressed because of injuries, but there was always someone to hold your hand. This is the first team that I truly like every man on it."

Then Russell joined his teammates in escorting the fully clothed Red Auerbach into his annual post-championship shower. "Last time in the shower for Red!" Bill yelled.

Next season player-coach William Felton Russell hopes to be escorted into the shower. Funny how things work out.

CAZZIE RUSSELL

The New York Knickerbockers, perennial losers in the National Basketball Association, were the biggest winners in the post-season college-player draft. The Knicks, who finished last in the East, had to win a coin toss with the Detroit Pistons, who were last in the West, for the right to select first in the draft. This was a lean year for college basketball stars, but it was a great year at the top. The best player in the country, everyone agreed, was the University of Michigan's two-time All-America and Player of the Year, Cazzie Russell. Piston owner Fred Zollner brought his own gold coin for the occasion, but Knick owner Ned Irish made the right call. It was a sad day for Zollner and a great day for the Irish. Not only did the Pistons desperately need a superstar for their under-manned team, they needed Cazzie—a big favorite in Detroit—for their gate.

Of course, Cazzie could make the Knicks a solid contender for the playoffs (something they haven't appeared in for years) in his very first season of pro ball. Said his coach, Dave Strack: "Cazzie is tough enough, big enough, strong enough, and smart enough for the pros. He has gone to the Piston games a lot this past season, and we have discussed the techniques of pro ball. He is a hard worker, and he learns quickly. I would be surprised if he wasn't as enthusiastic in pro ball as he was in college. He goes into everything that way."

Often the 6-5½, 220-pound Russell would work out on his own in the Michigan field house before games. Strack didn't think much of the idea, fearing it would tire him. But he let Cazzie have his way because Cazzie felt it was helping him. "He was right," Strack says.

Before the game with Bowling Green last season, for example, Cazzie didn't feel too good. He decided a workout would limber him up. He went into Yost Field House three hours before game time and got loose. Then he scored 22 points, led the team in rebounding and assists—as he did through the season—and the Wolverines won, 108-70.

Michigan, a losing basketball team before Russell's arrival on the scene, almost always won once he joined the varsity. There were other good players, of course; Bill Buntin, Oliver Darden, Bob Cantrel, John Clawson, John Thampson, Jim Myers. But first and foremost there was Cazzie Lee Russell, Jr.

As Michigan went on the road to play Wisconsin last January, Badger coach John Erickson said, "I doubt whether Michigan would have won the Big Ten title the last two years if it hadn't been for Cazzie's clutch performances. He has an unusual way of performing in the big games, and he has won many of them for the Wolverines by coming through at the right time.

"There are many other good players around the country, but there are few who can change defeat into victory like Russell. I can't pay him any higher tribute than that. For a powerful fellow, his moves are so fluid— like a player 5-10. And on top of the many things he does well, he seems to be a tremendous leader. This young man has intense desire and pride in his school. Whatever he does, he does with pride."

Which is why he practices so much and so intelligently. "I try to shoot every shot in workouts just like I'd do it in a game," Cazzie says. "That way you don't pick up any bad habits. I never let the ball go without figuring it's going through the hoop."

Usually it does, and particularly in clutch situations, as John Erickson pointed out. Strack was talking about his star's most brilliant performances after Russell's junior year when he selected five big games by Cazzie:

● Powerful Wichita State came into Detroit's Cobo Hall determined to hold down the high-scoring Wolverines. But Russell refused to be stopped. He scored 21 of the last 35 Michigan points, and there were less than three seconds on the clock when Cazzie went up for his final shot. It was a 25-foot jumper that won the game, 87-85.

● Underdog Princeton was on its way to an upset of Michigan until Bill Bradley fouled out—and Russell got hot—with five minutes to play. In the last two minutes

Cazzie brought his team from 11 points behind, then hit a 12-foot jump shot to win the game, 80-78.

● With Clyde Lee's Vanderbilt team leading with five minutes to play, Cazzie scored 11 points to bring Michigan the victory, 87-85.

● Illinois took the lead with a minute to play, but Cazzie scored to put Michigan ahead by one. Then he came back and hit on another jumper and followed it with a free throw as the Wolverines won, 80-79.

● With Indiana leading in overtime, Cazzie scored to tie the game at 92 with nine seconds left. In the second overtime, Russell's two free-throws with time running out won the game, 96-95.

Bill Buntin, the Michigan center, graduated before the '65–66 season, but that didn't keep Cazzie from taking the Wolverines to another Big Ten title. He did so with the same kind of heroics he'd displayed the previous year, only this time the team relied on him more than ever because of the loss of Buntin.

In the NCAA post-season tournament, Cazzie personally got the team into the regional finals. He had to win this one because he almost blew it. With Michigan ahead, 78-77, Cazzie slipped on the floor and lost the ball and Western Kentucky scored. Then Cazzie threw away a pass. Fortunately, Western Kentucky missed the subsequent foul shot, and Cazzie and Hilltopper Greg Smith both came down with the rebound. Then, when they went up for the jump ball, Smith fouled Cazzie, who said later: "Really quite an obvious foul" as he patted his bruised lip. There were 11 seconds on the clock when Russell went to the line, Michigan trailing, 79-78.

"I thought about those two dumb plays I'd just made when I lost the ball," Cazzie said in the locker room. "I said to myself: 'Take your time . . . you owe this to your team . . . and put a little arch on it.'"

"I never even considered that he might miss them," said smiling teammate Oliver Darden.

Cazzie didn't, and Michigan won. Actually, the Wolverine win was as much the result of Russell's feeding as his 24 points. Cazzie asked Strack at halftime if he could work from the top of the key as a passer in the second half since the Hilltoppers were ganging up on him. "I found I could be more valuable at the top," Russell said, "so I could look at everybody working against their zone defense. I fed off; I got more joy out of that. See, they concentrated on stopping me, and they left everyone else open." So Cazzie Russell, regular guard and occasional forward, played a high post and hit his teammates with passes.

However, that was Michigan's last victory of the season. Despite Russell's 29 points against Kentucky, the No. 1-ranked Wildcats won, 84-77. But Cazzie Lee Russell, Jr., had nothing to be ashamed of. In three years he had put the University of Michigan on the basketball map.

Before he arrived at Ann Arbor the athletic department virtually ignored basketball. No one went to the games, but who cared? That was the attitude. After all, the University sold 101,000 seats to each of its football games, why worry about filling 15,000 seats for basketball? But Dave Strack came to Michigan in 1960, and a few years later he brought in Cazzie Russell. Now Michigan is building a new field house. The once cellar-dwelling members of the Big Ten became a basketball power in the Big Ten.

Even athletic director Fritz Crisler became converted to the notion that a school can be strong in basketball as well as football. In fact, Crisler feels Russell is the greatest athlete he's ever seen at Michigan. "Fellow like him comes along once in a generation—maybe," Crisler said.

That is the attitude of pro basketball scouts on Cazzie Russell, too. Most of them say he can become another Oscar Robertson. Others say there will never be another Oscar Robertson. However, Cazzie was the nearest thing to Robertson in college since Oscar graduated from the University of Cincinnati in 1960. Russell's slightly taller and probably a bit stronger. There is some question about his being as quick as Robertson, and he'll certainly have to go some to develop the passing skills of Robertson.

But Cazzie may be as close as you can get to the Big O. The New York Knickerbockers of the NBA were happy to settle for the Big C. Fred Zollner of the Pistons now hates gold coins.

SATCH SANDERS

During the past decade the Boston Celtics dominated the National Basketball Association as no other team ever dominated a professional league. In recent years the Celtics' winning margin averaged as much as nine point a game. Last season Boston lost one of its top scorers when Tom Heinsohn retired, and it not only won fewer games, but it won by smaller margins. The winning average was down to 4.9 points per game. Naturally this put greater pressure on the team's defensive play. Tom (Satch) Sanders, Boston's outstanding defensive forward—the man whose job it is to guard the Elgin Baylors, the Jerry Lucases, and every other top shooting forward in the league—rose admirably to the challenge.

For the last five of his six seasons in the NBA, Sanders has been regarded as the toughest defensive forward in the league. He has not received a lot of recognition for his all-round skills because spectators are by and large not aware of them. But Sanders's play has not gone unnoticed by the men who try to score off him.

Jack Twyman, who was the Cincinnati Royal's shooting forward before Lucas joined the team, said last season: "I have to move more against Sanders to shake loose for a quick shot than against any other forward. Satch tries to cut me off from the ball. He is very effective at it."

Said Lucas: "More than anyone else in the league, Tom Sanders makes it hard for me to get the ball. Most defenders don't apply pressure until I have the ball. Not Sanders. He's always on top of me. He takes chances and guesses a lot about my moves. But he can afford to do this because [Bill] Russell is there to correct his mistakes. When he plays me close, I'll try to go around him and stop for a quick jump shot. I'll rarely try to go all the way because of Russell.

"But Sanders works harder on defense than any other forward."

106

Satch works harder on defense because that is his liveli-
hood, that is why the Celtics drafted him No. 1 in the
spring of 1960. Boston coach Red Auerbach saw the 6-6,
215-pound Sanders, who played center at New York University, three times and liked him. Of course, as usual the
Celtics had last draft choice, and all of the big-name ballplayers were gone when it was their turn. Still, Auerbach
said, "I figured if we could get Sanders to rebound a
little better and polish his shooting, he had a good chance.
He showed a lot of defensive ability."

Actually, one game was all Auerbach needed to see to
know that Sanders could make it in the pros even though
he wasn't voted to the All-America team. The game was
played in Charlotte, North Carolina, in March of 1960,
NYU vs. West Virginia in the Eastern Regionals of the
NCAA tournament. West Virginia, led by Jerry West—
who was justifiably voted to every All-America squad—had
beaten NYU earlier in the season, 98-69. But Satch Sanders
wouldn't let the Violets be beaten in this game. He scored
28 points and pulled down 19 rebounds as NYU won in
overtime, 82-81. He did more than that, though, on defense. He prevented West from winning the game for West
Virginia.

Jimmy Reiss scored what proved to be the winning
basket late in the overtime. Mountaineer coach Freddy
Schaus called time and gave the team the play for West.
His teammates set up for Jerry at midcourt and cleared the
middle lane. Meanwhile, Sanders stayed close to West,
keeping him outside. Then, with just 24 seconds on the
clock, Jerry started his drive, and the game came down to
a man-to-man battle between West and Sanders. Satch
pressed Jerry so tightly that the West Virginia star forced
his shot, and NYU won.

Afterward, Sanders said, "Man to man, West is the
toughest I've ever had to go against. I never had so much
pressure on me. I was saying a prayer I could stay with
him. I anticipated him going to the right, but he fooled
me and went to the left. But I'd been given him room,
figuring he'd have to go for the sure shot underneath. He
couldn't afford the jump shot then. I was in a spread stance,
and I was able to go with him. I arched my body to
force him away from the basket. It was the only thing to

do then, except pray. He had me so tired I couldn't do anything else."

Sanders had West tired, too, and it paid off. A few weeks later he was drafted by the Celtics, which didn't exactly make him happy. He had hoped to be drafted by the Knickerbockers, not only because he was a native New Yorker but because he knew he'd have a much better chance of making the Knicks. "I felt I wouldn't have a chance to make the club at Boston," Satch recalled later, "because there were too many good players there."

So Sanders signed with the Celtics and went out and bought himself a pair of contact lenses, on orders from Auerbach, to replace the steel-rimmed glasses he'd always worn in college ball. Red also told him to get rid of the knee pads he'd worn in college since they'd only slow him down.

"The contact lenses weren't as hard to get used to as I thought they'd be," Satch said. "And I did work out all summer in playgrounds. Then, in the exhibition games, Red played me a lot, and that's what helped me the most. And he worked very hard on me in practice."

Sanders had to make the always difficult switch from center to forward with the Celtics. "That was the hardest thing for me to learn this year," Satch said after his rookie season, "playing facing the basket. I'd never played outside before. I had to learn how to move, how to find shots, what to do with the ball, and how to make the shots."

As it turned out, he was lucky to go to the Celtics, who had clinched the Eastern title by January and could afford to give Sanders considerable playing time thereafter. He was especially impressive in the playoffs against Syracuse, holding down the scoring of Dolph Schayes, another former NYU star. Schayes later said, "I tried to induce the Nats to draft Sanders in '60. He played me great even as a rookie and is without doubt one of the most valuable Celtics."

Sanders averaged 5.3 points per game during his rookie season, and 8.9 points in the playoffs. Since then he has never averaged under 10.8 points per game in any season. Last year he increased his average to 12.6 points per game and pulled down 508 rebounds. He led the league in fouling out of games, with 19 disqualifications, and is always well up in that category as befits a hard-working defender.

The man Satch regards as hardest in the league to guard

is Elgin Baylor. "Elgin is my toughest assignment," he says. "He has strength, moves and the ability to hang in the air. I work hard to keep the ball away from him."

And Baylor? He says, "I'd say Sanders plays me tougher than anyone else. He's on me chest-to-chest every minute, always playing me to my right to make it tougher. And he's very fast and much stronger than he looks."

Alex Hannum seems to sum up Sanders's all-round ability and value best, saying, "I consider Sanders far and away the top defensive cornerman. Excellent on both boards and a good percentage shooter [slightly over .430 for his NBA career], he has a wonderfully balanced, all-round game. And with Bill Russell and K.C. Jones, he's the key to the Celtics' great defense."

Sanders is a quiet guy with a dry sense of humor. When people talk to him about his being one of the finest defensive players in the game, he says, "Believe me, that wasn't an easy reputation to come by. Why, I had to start the rumor myself."

In the off-season, the former baseball and basketball star at New York's Seward High School stays in very good shape in workouts with youngsters. Last summer he worked for the Boston Youth Activities Bureau conducting basketball clinics for boys. He's still a bachelor, and he enjoys the work. But he was a marketing major at NYU and plans eventually to enter the world of finance.

"Stocks and bonds sound like they might be fun," Satch says through a smile. "I hear a man can turn a tidy penny by just buying here, selling there."

Of course, Sanders's first interest is basketball. He plans to play seven or eight more years, and before last season he said, "The pressure is always on us, because everyone outside of Boston wants to see the Celtics lose. That's what makes it interesting to be a Celtic."

Last year opponents came close, but Sanders was a big reason they were unable to stop Boston from winning another championship. Satch's defense was essential, and he's always trying to improve it. "On defense," he says, "it's not so much a matter of working on skills, but of just plain working. But what's more important is keeping up with the new faces in the league and watching out for new tricks from old faces. You'll never learn them all, but you have to try to."

NATE THURMOND

Midway through the 1964-65 National Basketball Association season, the San Francisco Warriors traded Wilt Chamberlain. It shocked the world because Wilt is supposed to be one of those untradeable superstars. The Warriors said they could afford to make the deal because they had another young center who was playing out of position at forward, Nate Thurmond. They felt once Nate moved into his natural position, he would develop and become even more valuable than Wilt. Other NBA teams felt the same way apparently.

Said a Warrior spokesman after the trade: "We were offered more in players, more in cash, more in both for Thurmond than for Chamberlain. We could have kept both or we could have kept Wilt instead of Nate. We knew we were opening a hornet's nest by dealing Wilt. But we decided that if other clubs figured Thurmond would be worth more to them than Wilt, maybe we would not be so wrong in thinking so ourselves."

Thurmond had showed what he could do at center early in the season when he'd had to play there because of Chamberlain's illness. Nate averaged 21 points a game and led the league in rebounding for five games. Then, after Chamberlain had been traded, Thurmond averaged 22 points and 22 rebounds per game. This past season Nate, despite being troubled by a chronically bad back, averaged 18 rebounds (fourth best in the league) and 16.3 points. (Rookie-of-the-Year Rick Barry lowered Nate's totals in both categories with his contributions to the Warriors.)

San Francisco was very happy with the trade. Team owner Frank Mieuli said midway through this past season that he was more than happy. First, he felt Chamberlain didn't fit in with the style of play favored by coach Alex

Hannum (who, ironically, has since been fired by San Francisco and hired by Philadelphia to again coach Chamberlain). Said Mieuli: "We favor a style of play with running and motion, with a balanced offense and defense, and I knew that Thurmond could fit into that kind of game and Wilt couldn't. I also knew that Nate was five or six years younger than Wilt. And I was not unaware that Wilt commands a fabulous salary, but wasn't bringing any money back in as a home-court drawing card. Here in San Francisco, we have unusual civic pride and don't like second-hand heroes. Orlando Cepeda, who developed here is no Willie Mays, but he has always been more popular here than Mays, who is New York's hero. [Again, ironically, Cepeda was traded by the San Francisco Giants early this past baseball season, and the question of civic pride was not raised.] The fans here regard Thurmond as their own, not Chamberlain. And Alex Hannum thinks Thurmond can be the best center in the league in six or the next nine years, and feels he can build a winning team around him. I think we can build a whole new image around him."

As long as Nate's back holds up, that is. It originally acted up when Thurmond came down on an opponent's heel and wrenched the back after Chamberlain was traded. "The doctors at first figured it was a sprain or something," Nate said before last season, "but now they've decided that the tissues of the cartilage on the left side of my hip are dried out, that the accident only brought it to the surface, and that I may feel it from now on. I felt if I could rest for a couple of weeks I'd have been all right last season, but the team needed me so I kept playing. I rested this summer. I toured Europe during the summer with an NBA All-Star team, but the games were so easy I didn't have to extend myself. In one of the games we almost pitched a shutout. Don Ohl [of the Bullets] said the first guy to give up a bucket would have to buy sodas. Guess who gave up the first bucket? That's right, Nate Thurmond, the defensive star." Nate laughed.

He wasn't laughing when he tried the back out before the season, though. It was in a pick-up game with some other pros who live out on the West Coast. "It hurt like blazes," Nate said. "I feel bad about it. I'm afraid I'm just going to have to learn to live with it. It hurts worse when I make that quick, long leap to block a shot. I've tried corsets and elastic bandages, but they restrict me too much. The doctors say the only thing I can do for it is to take exercises to strengthen it."

Thurmond did just that, lifting weights regularly to build up his back. He found the workouts helped his appetite, and he began eating better, putting on solid weight that he felt would improve his stamina in games. "I'd like," he said, "to be able to play 48 minutes every game this season. I can learn to pace myself. Anyway, when I get tired, it only affects my shooting touch, not my rebounding or defense. When I sit on the bench, I cool off. Now that I'm in there [with the center job all to himself], I don't want to sit out."

He did sit out, though. Unfortunately, the back became so bad that he missed the last couple of weeks of the season. The Warriors had been battling for a spot in the playoffs, but without Thurmond they faltered, and St. Louis slipped by them at the end. The loss of Nate not only cost San Francisco a playoff berth, it also cost Alex Hannum—one of the finest coaches in the game—his job.

When the Warriors went into the NBA draft there were rumors that Thurmond's back injury might end his career, and that was why San Francisco was going to draft a big man to replace him. The rumors were untrue. Thurmond's back reportedly has responded well to treatment, and he is expected to be sound next season. The Warriors seem assured anyway, because they didn't draft a big man. They truly believe they've got the game's next great center.

Before the start of the '65–66 season Hannum was talking about Thurmond. "Nate is a complete player," Alex said, "who has all the skills John Kerr has—and he's my idea of a great all-around center. But Nate is naturally more talented than John and so he can become a much better player. He has to learn some of the cute maneuvers the great centers have. He has to get meaner out there. He's too nice a guy and doesn't want to make anyone mad at him. I don't believe you have to go to war and injure someone, but it's a rough game, and you have to be rough to protect yourself sometimes. Nate has the guts, I know. He played in such pain at times last season it was pathetic. He has the intelligence. If he dedicates himself to the job, and his back holds up, I think he can become the finest all-around center ever."

"Let's face it," Thurmond himself said, "I'm not Wilt Chamberlain, and I'm no Bill Russell. But I am Nate Thurmond, and maybe I can make that enough for anybody. You know something? I've led my teams in scoring only one or two years ever since I was in high school. I've never been all-anything that was important. I've always been behind someone. I'd like to be No. 1 for a change. I'd like my team to be No. 1 for a change."

Thurmond has worked very hard to come as far as he has in professional basketball. He grew up in Akron, Ohio, where his father worked in the Firestone plant. Nate played varsity basketball in high school, but he was no superstar. It didn't take him long to run through his college scholarship offers, and he accepted one to Bowling Green. At Akron Central High, Nate learned to play defense under coach Joe Siegfirth, and Bowling Green coach Harold Anderson liked this style of play in his big man, too. So Nate never averaged as much as 20 points a game in college, but he was always up among the nation's leading rebounders, and he was compared to Bill Russell for his shot-blocking ability on defense.

He was disappointed when San Francisco selected him in the draft because he didn't know what he could do with Wilt already stationed under the basket there. Nate had expected the Los Angeles Lakers to pick him. They were desperate for a center (and still are), and might have become a virtually unbeatable team with Thurmond (some people feel this is why the Warriors took Nate, just to block the Lakers and see what developed).

"I sure wish we would have gotten him," Laker coach Fred Schaus said last year. "Nate is a complete ballplayer. He's quicker and more agile and has longer arms than most men his size (6-11). Very few natural centers his size could have made the switch to a corner the way he did, particularly with a Chamberlain dominating the game at center. But Nate is unselfish and complemented Wilt very well. He didn't take bad shots—of course, he didn't have to shoot much with Wilt on the team. But he did get more than his share of rebounds. And he overpowered normal-sized forwards on defense. If his back holds up, I'm sure he can develop into an outstanding center because of his all-around ability. He has all the tools, he only needs experience. He can be great."

That, of course, is why the Warriors traded Chamberlain. Nate Thurmond is already a very good one, and if his back holds up he can be great.

JERRY WEST

In the March, 1962, issue of *Sport* Magazine, Arnold Hano predicted that Jerry West of Los Angeles Lakers would cease to be a superstar in five years. If he were still in the league, Hano wrote, he would be scoring something like eight points a game because West's frail physique would have been battered to the point where he could play only in spots by that time.

This point is raised here not only because Hano is one of the most perceptive writers around, but because many other knowledgeable people felt the same way he did about Jerry West. They didn't believe he could stand the grind. Not the way Jerry West plays basketball—which is as hard as he can go every instant he's on the floor.

By 1962 Jerry had already suffered a broken nose four times playing basketball, among other assorted injuries. The nose breaks, combined with his sinus condition and the smoky arenas he plays basketball in, make breathing a real problem for Jerry West. Particularly when he's running all-out for some 40 minutes during a game. West's other injuries have included a broken thumb and torn hamstring, which sidelined him for 32 games, and a finger in the eye that benched him for a game last season. And he has played with numerous injuries and ignored them. At one time Laker coach Fred Schaus announced that Jerry would be out with a sprained ankle, yet West scored 30 points on that sprained ankle. Another time Jerry told his wife he would miss a game because of a bad cold (he is plagued by bad colds the way garlic fanciers are plagued by bad breath), yet West scored 35 points with that bad cold.

Still, despite his injuries, despite the fact that at 6-3 and 178 pounds Jerry West was not expected by many people to still be a superstar in the rugged NBA at age

27, he is. He is, in fact, better now than he ever was. Last season Jerry scored more points (2,476), had a higher average (31.4 points per game), had more assists (480), and a higher free-throw percentage (.860) than ever before. He finished second in the league in scoring, fourth in assists, fourth in free-throw percentage, and ninth in field-goal percentage.

How come he's still around?

"I guess I've matured," Jerry said last season. "That's the reason I haven't worn out physically. I'm bigger and stronger today than when I broke in. I was 21 years old when I came up, and I was a skinny kid."

Now he's all of eight pounds heavier than he was at age 21. Perhaps Laker general manager Lou Mohs made the most telling point about West's injuries when he said, "Jerry gets hurt not because he's frail, but because he goes all-out and takes chances others won't take." His slim build has nothing to do with his injuries. But the fact that he has survived does have to do with the maturity West talks about. "I am learning to cope with this game," he says. What he means is that he *has* learned to cope with it.

"I have a better *feel* of the game," he says. I have learned how to make my shot and not get hurt. I can find the position to make my shot without getting hurt."

When he was younger and breaking his nose as a matter of course, West used to regularly drive down the middle. Or try to. Something told him finally this was not the thing to do. His nose, no doubt. For large bodies lurk in that lane, towering 6-8, 6-10, 7-1. And parts of those large bodies had a habit of landing on Jerry West's nose. Then Jerry realized that for the most part not only was it silly to keep driving down bloody-nose lane, it was unnecessary.

West is a great outside shooter, the very best in the game. What's more, he gets his shots off so quickly, from so many different angles and with so many arch variations, that he is impossible to stop. There are those who claim no one is impossible to stop. Get a couple of good defenders, even fair defenders, and have them do nothing except hound a guy like Jerry West, alternate fresh men playing right in his face, and he will be stopped. Now, by stopped you mean holding Jerry West to 20 points or under, for this is stopping him. But we saw West against the New York Knickerbockers last season. Coach Dick McGuire assigned Howard Komives and Emmette Bryant to take turns guarding West. Neither is a super defender in the K. C. Jones mold, but each is fast, tenacious, and a hustler who hates to be scored on. Late in the game we remarked that they were doing a good job on West. Tom Panagakos, the unofficial basketball mayor of Madison Square Garden, said, "It looks like it because they're working so hard on him, but West's still getting off his shots. They're keeping a hand in his face or on his jersey, but wait. He'll still end up with 35 points." West ended up with 42 points. He is unstoppable.

His Laker teammates work for him, and Jerry has learned how to slip behind that screen from Ruby La-Russo or Darrell Imhoff . . . or anyone he can get behind wearing a Los Angeles jersey . . . and pop the ball into the basket before his defender can get around the screen. He is so quick. He brings the ball up, tosses it to Walt Hazzard, darts behind Elgin Baylor, takes the return pass, and the ball is up, the two points on the scoreboard. Just pass, dart, catch, pop.

Yet pro basketball has taken its toll on West. "You reach a certain stage," he told Arnold Hano, who happily withdrew his earlier prediction about Jerry, last season, "where the pressure piles up until you are not able to do your best. You can't concentrate all the time. You can't get up for every minute of every game. You can't get up for every game. Maybe you can get up for two games out of three."

That's 60 out of 80 regular-season games. For anyone who watches pro basketball consistently, this estimate seems just about right.

"You know what's really awful?" Jerry says. "Those last ten to 15 games every season. If your team is out of the standings, it's tough to play useless games. If you're way ahead, you've got little incentive. Those games are useless, too. Individual team pride in those last ten or 15 games dictates which team will win."

That's one thing the Lakers have. Coach Fred Schaus sees to that. He drives his teams, even scrimmages them between games during the season when they're not going well, or when he feels improvements can be made. But he doesn't do this for Jerry West, he doesn't have to drive West. Jerry has the pride. He has ambitions of his own.

Lou Mohs once told writer Bill Libby: "West wants to be financially independent by the time he is 40, which is a laudable ambition. He also wants to be the greatest small man ever to play this game, which he may already be. He sets high standards and goes after them fiercely."

His family in Cabin Creek, West Virginia, was not wealthy, but this has not kept him from wanting to be. Basketball earned him a scholarship to the University of West Virginia, and he earned All-America honors there and a good contract with the Lakers. When he came into the pros he, admittedly, was not a good ballhandler and he was not an outstanding dribbler, two abilities you normally find in a guard. But that was six years ago. Now West is a capable ballhandler and a very good dribbler, though he still denies being proficient in either category. He does not deny that he is worth the estimated $55,000 he earns annually from the Lakers, though.

He used to have a difficult time negotiating contracts when Bob Short owned the team, though the Lakers were the most successful club in the league at the box office. Now Jack Kent Cooke owns the team, and Jerry says, "I am very fond of our owner, Mr. Cooke. I was not so fond of the former owner, Bob Short. I don't think I was treated very fairly by the old regime. Now I am."

He is disappointed that his team has never won the NBA championship. The Lakers took the Celtics through seven games again last season before losing the playoffs. However, Jerry West says he would like to play ten years in the NBA before quitting, which will give him four more shots at the title. And ten years is five more than many people gave Jerry West when he came into the NBA.

The Coaches

Dave DeBusschere: When the Chicago White Sox were the only team willing to sign Dave DeBusschere to a $70,000 baseball contract and still allow him to play professional basketball, too, Ed Short said, "We weren't hot about the basketball deal, either. We hope to talk him out of that end of it after a year or two." Yet young Dave DeBusschere went on to become not only an NBA star but a coach as well, and then he talked himself out of the baseball end of it. He took over the Pistons in 1964–65 when they had a 2-11 record. The team did much better under his leadership, winning 29 of its remaining 69 games. The main thing he did was install a free-lance offense in place of Charley Wolf's more patterned style of play. But this past season it wouldn't have mattered what Dave did—unless he could grow four or five inches and play center. Without a good big man and without high-scoring Terry Dischinger, the Pistons won only 22 of 58 games. Still lacking a good big man, DeBusschere's prospects for this season look no brighter. "I told the other players," Dave said after he took over the Pistons, "that I'm not going to be a great strategy man. A Schaus, a Hannum, and an Auerbach know more about basketball and substituting players than I'll ever learn." Even a Schaus, a Hannum, and an Auerbach couldn't help the Pistons in their present circumstances. Fortunately, Dave's playing skills are too outstanding for him to lose his job on the court even if he should lose it on the bench.

Mike Farmer: A player for the St. Louis Hawks until early last season, when Mike Farmer was taken off the active list he became a Hawk scout. He found himself in a peculiar position last spring. The Bullets were in a peculiar position, too, once Paul Seymour abruptly announced he would not coach in Baltimore this season. Why he quit has never been fully explained, but he quit, and the management of the Baltimore team began a rapid search for a replacement before the upcoming draft of college players. They settled on Farmer, who did not apply for the job but who was nevertheless anxious to try coaching professionally. However, Mike said, "This is a unique situation because I am still under obligation to Ben Kerner in St. Louis and will remain available to assist the Hawks in next month's draft of college players. But I think what I've had to say about the draft up until now will be my main contribution to the Hawks." He could not confer with Bullet general manager Buddy Jeannette, though. "In all honesty," Mike said, "I don't think I can." He didn't but became the Bullet coach anyway, the team's fourth in as many years in Baltimore. He was preceded by Bob Leonard, Jeannette, and Seymour. Farmer's playing career began with the New York Knicks and took him to the American Basketball League before he finished up with the Hawks. The 30-year-old former defensive specialist played college ball at the University of San Francisco with Bill Russell of the Celtics, who also starts a pro coaching career this season. Russell starts with something Farmer doesn't have, of course—a player like Bill Russell.

Richie Guerin: The former New York Knickerbocker All-Star was telling everyone all through last season that it would be his last as a player-coach. In fact, Richie said it was impossible for anyone to do an outstanding job of coaching as a player. But Guerin did exactly that in 1964–65 and in 1965–66. He replaced Harry Gallatin halfway through the schedule two years ago and got the St. Louis Hawks into the playoffs. And he did so despite the absence of Bob Pettit much of the time, because of injuries. This past season Pettit was absent all of the time, having retired. Guerin had a lot of problems, particularly in his backcourt depth, but he again led the Hawks into the playoffs. He had to play in each of the 80 regular-season games to do so, and he did an excellent job, scoring, 1,190 points and making 388 assists. Perhaps he played too well, because just before the NBA draft the Hawks announced that Guerin was not retiring. It was strange, because in order for Richie to remain on the active list, another St. Louis player had to be made available to the newly formed Chicago Bulls team. The man grabbed up by the Bulls was young cornerman Jim Washington, who was highly regarded by most people in the NBA. Apparently he wasn't as highly regarded by Hawk owner Ben Kerner as Richie Guerin the player. So Richie will play and coach once more.

Alex Hannum: Hannum has been known as one of the best coaches in the NBA since he took over the Syracuse Nationals some ten years ago. But he was fired by San Francisco Warrior owner Frank Mieuli last season, reportedly because Alex didn't stay in San Francisco 12 months of the year. Hannum himself said, "I am basically a basketball man who puts the game of basketball first, pro basketball next, and the franchise third. They [the Warriors] are a promotional-type management. There was a difference in philosophy." The Warriors are trying to build a following, and there are many ways to do so, but the only one that interested Hannum was on the basketball court, not in promotions. Still, Alex wasn't long without a job. The Philadelphia 76ers fired Dolph Schayes and hired Hannum. Alex made sure his old friend Schayes was gone under any circumstances before he accepted the job. One of the first things Hannum did then was meet with Wilt Chamberlain, who had been traded from the Warriors while Alex was coaching them and was severely hurt by being dealt away. Hannum says Wilt knew he had nothing to do with the trade. "We talked about the past, and we talked about the future," Alex said. "Wilt is a headline-getting character, no mistake about that, and he has to realize he's a target. They got to blame someone when the team doesn't win so they blame him." Alex tried to make Chamberlain see that he had to accept this and just play his game. But Hannum plans, with Wilt's help, to see that the 76ers don't lose this season, and then Chamberlain won't have to worry about being a scapegoat.

Johnny Kerr: For several months before the Chicago
Bulls selected their players from those made available by
the other teams, it was rumored that DePaul coach Ray
Meyer would be hired by the NBA's newest team. Whether
he turned down the job or not isn't known. But Bulls'
owner Dick Klein made no mistake in the man he did
hire to coach his team, veteran center Johnny Kerr. Only
this past season the 33-year-old Kerr set the record for
most consecutive games played in the NBA (917—from
October 31, 1954, to November 4, 1965). Red Kerr is
known as one of the most intelligent players in the game,
and he also possesses one of sport's finest senses of humor.
He will need both these qualities in his first season as a
coach. He did not get what you could call an exceptional
squad, even as expansion teams go. Kerr did get a highly
regarded assistant coach in his old friend and teammate
from the Syracuse Nationals and Philadelphia 76ers, Al
Bianchi. A graduate of the University of Illinois and
native of Chicago, Kerr said on becoming coach: "This
definitely will be a tough job, but between Bianchi, Klein,
and myself, we hope to restore pro basketball interest
here."

Dick McGuire: His former coach at St. John's and with
the Knicks, Joe Lapchick, calls Dick McGuire "an accident they came to appreciate at St. John's." Dick was
never even a starting ballplayer in high school, and Lapchick gave him a scholarship to St. John's only because
Joe wanted his younger brother, Al, for the university
later. Dick, of course, went on to become a five-time NBA
All-Star with the Knicks, finished his career in Detroit,
and ended up coaching the Pistons. McGuire led that
lackluster team in the playoffs in each of his four seasons
in Detroit, then quit because he wasn't spending enough
time with his family in Huntington, New York. When the
Knicks got off to another bad start under Harry Gallatin
last season despite the addition of two superstars in Dick
Barnett and Walt Bellamy, team president Ned Irish went
after McGuire. Dick, who hadn't been happy selling insurance, was anxious to get back into pro basketball
if he could coach in New York. Lapchick said, "He has
a great understanding of guys and their attitudes. My only

fear is that this understanding be taken for weakness. Those years in Detroit had to toughen him up." And Al McGuire, now the coach at Marquette, said, "Dick had to get back into basketball. Guys loved playing with him, and they'll play for him. If given material in the area you play against, he's going to win. Dick's assets are the basics: getting the most out of his players and not over-coaching. That's got to be enough."

Jack McMahon: "What kind of coach would I be if I wasn't confident we can win all the time?" Jack McMahon asked rhetorically after his Cincinnati Royals had played so badly just before the playoffs. Well, McMahon is confident his team can win all the time, and he had his team believing it, too, when the Royals won two of the first three playoff games with the Celtics. Unfortunately, the Royals couldn't win one more game, but it was through no fault of McMahon's. He made excellent matchups against the Celtics, pulling little Adrian Smith every time K. C. Jones was out of the Boston lineup and playing either Tom Thacker or Jon McGlocklin against the bigger Celtic guards, Sam Jones and John Havlicek. The only matchup he couldn't make was a man to handle Bill Russell, and that was the difference in the series. McMahon has ballooned since his playing days as a star guard in Rochester and St. Louis, but he has mellowed somewhat. He still argues with referees when he feels it's necessary, but he hasn't thrown a basketball at an official since 1956. Jack's confident, though, that if he did so today he could still hit him.

Bill Russell: In his fascinating autobiography *Go Up to Glory*, which he wrote with Bill McSweeny, Bill Russell says, "One might say my personal relationship with Red Auerbach can only be considered cordial. In my opinion the man is a genius in sports. He is not always right. He is an egotist who has a terrible temper, and he is a man who can go off the deep end sometimes. He can be as gruff and as nasty and as miserable a human being as you want to meet. Conversely, he can be quiet, peaceful, and a decent guy." Many of the same things can be said about

Bill Russell, who has a lot of respect for Auerbach and who receives a lot of respect from Auerbach. This is why these two highly individual personalities worked so well together as coach and player and why they should work well together as general manager and player-coach. After he was named coach, Russell said, "I can't retire. The coach wouldn't approve. I can't get tired. The coach won't allow it. I am like Red. I'm a hard-head, too. I've seen the aggravation and frustration that Red has gone through for the last ten years, but being sort of a nut myself . . . I thought it might be fun." There will be fun for Bill Russell in his first season as a coach, but there will be aggravation and frustration as well. There may even be disappointment, because the Celtics have more problems and tougher competition now than they've had in years. But it will be interesting for Russell and for fans. Bill Russell always makes things interesting on a basketball court, and off of it as well, when he's of a mind to.

Bill Sharman: After breaking into professional basketball with the Washington Capitols, Bill Sharman played ten years with the Boston Celtics and led the team in scoring four times. He is regarded as the greatest foul shooter in the history of the game, hitting 88 per cent of his freethrows through an 11-year career. He holds the record for freethrow percentage, having hit on 93 per cent of his shots in 1958–59 and on 92 per cent in his last year in the league, 1960–61. He then became a player-coach for the short-lived Los Angeles Jets of the American Basketball League. When they folded, he took over the Cleveland Pipers and led them to the ABL championship. Like Dave DeBusschere and Gene Conley, Sharman was a pro baseball player at the same time he was starring in basketball. Bill played several years of Triple A ball in the Dodger organization and was even on the Brooklyn bench when Bobby Thompson hit the dramatic home run that won the pennant for the Giants. When he saw he wasn't going to make it to the big leagues, though, Sharman concentrated on basketball. After the ABL disbanded, Bill coached Los Angeles State for a couple of years, then joined the Tidewater Oil Company promotion staff and became a radio and TV color announcer for Hawk and

Celtic games. But despite turning down other coaching offers since, he was happy when the San Francisco Warrior job was offered him.

Fred Schaus: There were many rumors at the end of last season that if Fred Schaus did not bring a championship back to Los Angeles he would be fired. Although the rumors came from excellent sources, they were unsubstantiated. Schaus was rehired, and rightly so. He should have been given a sizable raise for the job he does with the Lakers year after year, getting them into the championship finals and then doing so well against the Boston Celtics without a big man. The Celtics, of course, have had the best big man in the game until last year, Bill Russell. Yet Schaus's Lakers have played the Celtics virtually even. The Lakers took the Celtics to seven games again in the spring of '66 and could easily have won had they not shot so incredibly bad in that final playoff game. It was Schaus who came up with an excellent gimmick in the playoffs to offset Boston's manpower advantage. A good deal of the time he played two other guards with Jerry West and Elgin Baylor, overcoming his height deficit with speed and skillful shooting. Schaus is, to put it mildly, a most able basketball coach. He has been ever since the Laker management hired him away from the University of West Virginia. Los Angeles has never been out of the playoffs under his guidance.

THE PRO OFFENSES

The offenses in professional basketball are strikingly simple compared to those in pro football. Basically, the coaches around the league have the same idea. They each have specialists on their teams that do certain things well, and these specialties are what the coaches try to take advantage of. Since basketball is first of all a running game, the coaches try to have their teams run as much as possible—beat the other team to the basket, get down there before the opposition can get back on defense. When this doesn't work, and it doesn't when the team gets tired, then set plays are attempted.

These usually involve "picking" off an opponent, which is blocking him out to allow the man he is guarding to get free for a shot. The "pick" also forces opponents to switch defensive assignments, the idea being to get a weak defender on a top shooter or to cause a mismatch in size. The mismatch occurs when a small man must cover a big man in close to the basket, and the big man's height allows him to shoot over the little man. A mismatch also occurs when a big man has to guard a smaller and quicker man who has room to maneuver past the big man for an easy shot. If a great shooter—and they come in all sizes in professional basketball—gets even a foot of daylight around the basket, he's going to score at least 50 per cent of the time. In fact, if given room, most NBA players can hit close to 40 per cent of their shots from almost any place on the court. So plays are designed to give them room to shoot, as the following diagrams show:

SIMPLE PICK FOR A GUARD

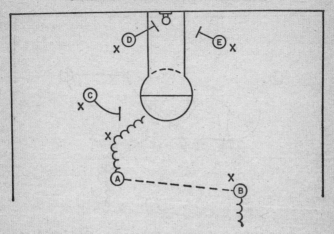

B brings the ball up court and passes to A, who simply drives his man into the pick set by C's stepping over. A then darts to his right and pops up a jump shot as D and E move in for a possible rebound or tap-in.

> **KEY:** Solid line—path of player
> Wavy line—dribble
> Broken line—pass

DOUBLE PICK FOR A FORWARD

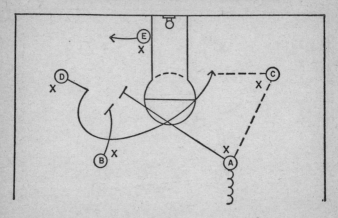

A dribbles the ball down and passes to C. Then A and B break to the opposite side of the court and set a double pick for D, who cuts around them to the middle for a pass from C. D either shoots or drives in for a layup if the lane is open.

> **KEY:** Solid line—path of player
> Wavy line—dribble
> Broken line—pass

CLEAR-OUT FOR A GUARD

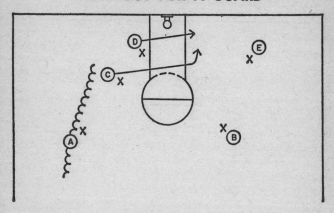

When you have a guard like Jerry West or Oscar Robertson or Dick Barnett, this is a most effective play. The shooting guard, A, merely dribbles down and as he approaches the top of the key, the forward and center, C and D, cut across the court to clear out that side for him. A then can work one-on-one with his defender from close range.

> KEY: Solid line—path of player
> Wavy line—dribble
> Broken line—pass

GUARD OPTION

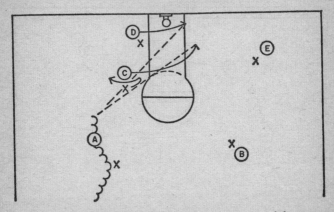

If A gets by his defender instantly with a quick move, the man guarding C (or even the man guarding D) will have to drop off to pick up A. Then A has the option of passing to his forward, C, or his center, D, for an open shot.

KEY: Solid line—path of player
Wavy line—dribble
Broken line—pass

PICK FOR A CENTER

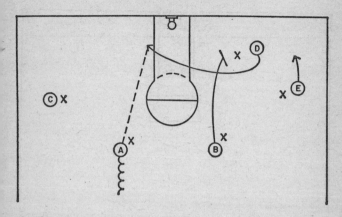

As guard A dribbles in, his backcourt partner, B, races toward the basket to pick for the center, D, who cuts around the pick (the man guarding him should bump into B). Player A then can hit D with a pass for an easy shot.

KEY: Solid line—path of player
Wavy line—dribble
Broken line—pass

OUT-OF-BOUNDS PLAY

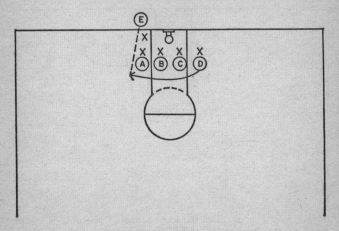

This is a widely used out-of-bounds play right under the basket. Players, A, B, C, and D line up shoulder to shoulder and D, a speedy guard, darts around behind the picks set by A, B and C, takes the pass-in from E, and pops.

KEY: Solid line—path of player
Wavy line—dribble
Broken line—pass

The Statistics

NATIONAL BASKETBALL ASSOCIATION

FINAL STANDINGS

1965-66 SEASON

	Phil	Bos	Cln	NY	LA	Balt	St.L.	SF	Det	W	L	Pct.	Scoring For	Agst.
EASTERN DIVISION														
Philadelphia	—	6	6	8	8	5	7	8	7	55	25	.688	9387	9013
Boston	4	—	5	10	7	7	7	8	6	54	26	.675	9014	8623
Cincinnati	4	5	—	7	4	7	5	5	8	45	35	.563	9424	9331
New York	2	0	3	—	5	3	4	5	8	30	50	.375	9335	9543
WESTERN DIVISION														
Los Angeles	2	3	6	5	—	6	8	7	8	45	35	.563	9557	9309
Baltimore	5	3	3	6	4	—	6	6	5	38	42	.475	9465	9560
St. Louis	3	3	5	6	2	4	—	6	7	36	44	.450	8913	8958
San Francisco	2	2	5	5	3	4	4	—	9	35	45	.438	9243	9455
Detroit	3	4	2	2	2	5	3	1	—	22	58	.275	8827	9373

NBA CHAMPIONSHIP FINAL

LOS ANGELES

	m	fgm	fga	ftm	fta	reb	a	pf	pts
Baylor	45	6	22	6	6	14	1	1	18
West	48	12	27	12	16	10	3	3	36
Ellis	34	5	11	2	3	11	0	2	12
Goodrich	30	2	9	2	4	4	1	4	6
King	16	1	4	0	1	2	0	1	2
Boozer	4	0	0	0	0	2	1	1	0
Hazzard	23	5	7	2	5	2	3	2	12
Imhoff	14	0	1	0	0	3	0	3	0
LaRusso	25	2	7	3	4	6	0	5	7
Totals	240	33	88	27	38	60	9	22	93

BOSTON

	m	fgm	fga	ftm	fta	reb	a	pf	pts
Sanders	31	3	9	1	1	4	3	5	7
Havlicek	48	6	21	4	6	16	2	3	16
Russell	48	10	22	5	5	32	1	5	25
K. C. Jones	31	2	9	1	1	2	3	5	5
S. Jones	29	10	21	2	2	5	0	5	22
Naulls	3	0	1	0	0	1	0	3	0
Nelson	28	2	9	4	4	0	2	3	6
Siegfried	22	4	13	4	5	2	2	4	12
Totals	240	37	105	21	24	77	13	33	95
Los Angeles			20		18		22		33—93
BOSTON			27		26		23		19—95

NBA PLAYOFF LEADERS

Most Points—J. West, LA, 479
Best Average Per Game—J. West, LA, 34.2
Best Field Goal Percentage (25 or more) J. West, LA, .518
Best Free Throw Percentage (25 or more) C. Hagan, St.L., .926
Most Rebounds—B. Russell, Bos., 428
Most Assists—J. West, LA, 79
Most Personal Fouls Committed—T. Sanders, Bos., 70
Most Points Scored in One Game—W. Chamberlain, Phil., Bos @ Phil 4/12, 46
Best Free Throw Percentage in One Game—O. Robertson, Cin., Bos @ Cin, 3/26, 13-13

TEAM PLAYOFF STATISTICS

	G	Field Goals			Free Throws			Miscellaneous				Scoring Average		
		Made	Att.	Pct.	Made	Att.	Pct.	Rbnd	Asst	PF	D*	For	Agst	Dif.
Boston	17	735	1691	.435	499	651	.767	1153	368	484	5	115.8	110.2	5.6
Los Angeles	14	633	1363	.464	367	476	.771	768	311	358	3	116.6	116.3	0.3
St. Louis	10	432	966	.447	276	371	.744	597	251	247	3	114.0	115.4	—1.4
Cincinnati	5	196	462	.424	159	199	.799	314	79	142	4	110.2	114.8	—4.6
Baltimore	3	134	288	.465	55	90	.611	188	54	92	6	107.7	113.0	—5.3
Philadelphia	5	194	502	.386	132	203	.650	361	96	143	3	104.0	113.6	—9.6

Eastern Division Semi-Finals Series
Boston defeated Cincinnati 3 games to 2

W Mar 23 Cincinnati 107 @ Boston 103
Sa Mar 26 Boston 132 @ Cincinnati 125
Su Mar 27 Cincinnati 113 @ Boston 107
W Mar 30 Boston 120 @ Cincinnati 103
Fr Apr 1 Cincinnati 103 @ Boston 112

Eastern Division Final Series
Boston defeated Philadelphia 4 games to 1

Su Apr 3 Boston 115 @ Philadelphia 96
W Apr 6 Philadelphia 93 @ Boston 114
Th Apr 7 Boston 105 @ Philadelphia 111
Su Apr 10 Philadelphia 108 @ Boston 114 OT
Tu Apr 12 Boston 120 @ Philadelphia 112

Western Division Semi-Final Series
St. Louis defeated Baltimore 3 to 0

Th Mar 24 St. Louis 113 @ Baltimore 111
Su Mar 27 St. Louis 105 @ Baltimore 100
W Mar 30 Baltimore 112 @ St. Louis 121

Western Division Final Series
Los Angeles defeated St. Louis 4 games to 3

Fr Apr 1 St. Louis 106 @ Los Angeles 129
Su Apr 3 St. Louis 116 @ Los Angeles 125
W Apr 6 Los Angeles 113 @ St. Louis 120
Sa Apr 9 Los Angeles 107 @ St. Louis 95
Su Apr 10 St. Louis 112 @ Los Angeles 100
W Apr 13 Los Angeles 127 @ St. Louis 131
Fr Apr 15 St. Louis 121 @ Los Angeles 130

*—Number of games disqualified on Personal Fouls

TEAM PLAYOFF STATISTICS (Cont'd)

Championship Series
Boston defeated Los Angeles 4 games to 3

```
Su Apr 17  Los Angeles 133  @  Boston      129 OT
Tu Apr 19  Los Angeles 109  @  Boston      129
W  Apr 20  Boston      120  @  Los Angeles 106
Fr Apr 22  Boston      122  @  Los Angeles 117
Su Apr 24  Los Angeles 121  @  Boston      117
Tu Apr 26  Boston      115  @  Los Angeles 123
Th Apr 28  Los Angeles  93  @  Boston       95
```

INDIVIDUAL PLAYOFF STATISTICS

	G	Min-utes	FG Made	FG Att.	FG Pct.	Ft. Made	Ft. Att.	Ft. Pct.	Re-bnd	As-sist	Per Fls.	D*	Tot. Pts.	Avg. Pts.
BALTIMORE														
D. Ohl	3	111	34	67	.507	12	16	.750	14	8	13	1	80	26.7
B. Howell	3	94	23	50	.460	8	11	.727	30	2	13	1	54	18.0
J. Egan	3	117	20	47	.404	10	16	.625	9	23	14	0	48	16.0
J. Green	3	96	20	34	.588	1	8	.125	27	4	9	2	41	13.7
J. Barnes	3	93	16	32	.500	7	13	.538	28	3	15	0	39	13.0
B. Ferry	3	82	11	20	.550	9	13	.692	25	5	10	2	31	10.3
J. Sloan	2	34	5	12	.417	3	4	.750	16	1	6	1	13	6.5
J. K. Loughery	3	27	3	7	.429	3	6	.500	1	6	4	0	9	3.0
J. Kerr	3	49	2	11	.182	1	2	.500	17	4	5	0	5	1.7
G. Johnson	1	8	1	4	.250	0	0	.000	0	0	1	0	2	2.0
B. Warley	2	9	0	4	.000	1	1	1.000	2	0	2	0	1	0.5
	G	Min-utes	FG Made	FG Att.	FG Pct.	Ft. Made	Ft. Att.	Ft. Pct.	Re-bnd	As-sist	Per Fls.	D*	Tot. Pts.	Avg. Pts.
BOSTON														
S. Jones	17	602	154	343	.449	114	136	.838	86	53	65	1	422	24.8
J. Havlicek	17	719	153	374	.409	95	113	.841	154	70	69	1	401	23.6
B. Russell	17	814	124	261	.475	76	123	.618	428	85	60	0	324	19.1
T. Sanders	17	500	97	201	.483	36	48	.750	119	27	70	2	230	13.5
L. Siegfried	17	452	81	193	.420	62	75	.827	42	41	52	0	224	13.2
D. Nelson	17	316	50	118	.424	42	52	.808	85	13	50	0	142	8.4
K. C. Jones	17	543	45	109	.413	39	57	.684	52	75	65	0	129	7.6
M. Counts	10	82	14	39	.359	15	17	.882	40	3	26	0	43	4.3
W. Naulls	11	75	9	35	.257	17	21	.810	16	1	23	0	35	3.2
R. Bonham	5	16	7	11	.636	3	9	.333	4	0	2	0	17	3.4
J. Thompson	3	11	1	7	.143	0	0	.000	3	0	2	0	2	0.7

CINCINNATI	G	Minutes	FG Made	FG Att.	FG Pct.	Ft. Made	Ft. Att.	Ft. Pct.	Rebnd	Assist	Per Fls.	D*	Tot. Pts.	Avg. Pts.
O. Robertson	5	224	49	120	.408	61	68	.897	38	39	20	1	159	31.8
J. Lucas	5	231	40	85	.471	27	35	.771	101	14	14	0	107	21.4
H. Hairston	5	150	25	62	.403	27	38	.711	37	13	20	1	77	15.4
A. Smith	5	157	22	59	.373	21	22	.955	12	12	12	0	65	13.0
W. Embry	5	139	16	38	.421	7	12	.583	34	2	23	2	39	7.8
J. McGlocklin	4	66	14	29	.483	2	2	1.000	8	4	11	0	30	7.5
C. Dierking	4	64	9	18	.500	9	10	.900	15	1	11	0	27	6.8
T. Hawkins	5	109	11	24	.458	1	6	.167	22	5	16	0	23	4.6
J. Thacker	4	46	7	22	.318	3	4	.750	9	5	11	0	17	4.3
J. Twyman	2	11	2	4	.500	1	2	.500	2	0	3	0	5	2.5
G. Wilson	1	3	1	1	1.000	0	0	.000	1	0	1	0	2	2.0

*—Number of games disqualified on personal fouls.

LOS ANGELES	G	Minutes	FG Made	FG Att.	FG Pct.	Ft. Made	Ft. Att.	Ft. Pct.	Rebnd	Assist	Per Fls.	D*	Tot. Pts.	Avg. Pts.
J. West	14	619	185	357	.518	109	125	.872	88	79	40	3	479	34.2
E. Baylor	14	586	145	328	.442	85	105	.810	197	52	38	0	375	26.8
R. LaRusso	14	397	57	124	.460	53	67	.791	99	26	47	0	167	11.9
W. Hazzard	14	340	70	142	.493	26	42	.619	41	44	40	0	166	11.9
L. Ellis	14	426	56	138	.406	25	39	.641	133	8	52	1	137	9.8
G. Goodrich	11	290	43	92	.467	29	43	.674	42	33	35	0	115	10.5
J. King	13	287	35	84	.417	12	17	.706	33	31	40	1	82	6.3
B. Boozer	10	181	26	65	.400	15	20	.750	50	7	20	0	67	6.7
D. Imhoff	14	243	14	40	.350	13	18	.722	81	30	42	1	41	2.9
T. Hoover	4	11	2	3	.667	0	0	.000	3	1	3	0	4	1.0
G. Wiley	2	5	0	1	.000	0	0	.000	1	0	1	0	0	0.0

	G	Min-utes	FG Made	FG Att.	FG Pct.	Ft. Made	Ft. Att.	Ft. Pct.	Re-bnd	As-sist	Per Fls.	D*	Tot. Pts.	Avg. Pts.
PHILADELPHIA														
W. Chamberlain	5	240	56	110	.509	28	68	.412	151	15	10	0	140	28.0
H. Greer	5	226	32	91	.352	18	23	.783	36	21	21	0	82	16.4
C. Walker	5	181	24	64	.375	25	31	.806	37	15	18	0	73	14.6
W. Jones	5	156	25	77	.325	15	22	.682	15	18	18	2	65	13.0
L. Jackson	5	163	21	49	.429	18	22	.818	44	8	21	1	60	12.0
A. Bianchi	5	64	18	43	.419	9	12	.750	10	4	19	0	45	9.0
D. Gambee	5	82	11	29	.379	8	11	.727	14	4	14	0	30	6.0
B. Cunningham	4	69	5	31	.161	11	13	.846	18	10	11	0	21	5.3
G. Ward	5	44	2	8	.250	0	1	.000	5	1	11	0	4	0.8
ST. LOUIS														
R. Guerin	10	399	72	159	.453	62	76	.816	37	79	41	0	206	20.6
B. Bridges	10	421	86	170	.506	31	43	.721	149	28	47	0	203	20.3
Z. Beaty	10	418	73	148	.493	44	58	.759	131	22	38	0	190	19.0
J. Caldwell	10	315	78	169	.462	31	49	.633	55	16	29	0	187	18.7
L. Wilkens	10	391	57	143	.399	57	83	.687	54	70	43	0	171	17.1
C. Hagan	10	200	44	97	.454	25	27	.926	34	18	15	0	113	11.3
R. Thorn	7	119	12	39	.308	14	18	.778	17	10	9	0	38	3.8
P. Silas	7	80	5	18	.278	8	11	.727	34	2	11	0	18	2.6
G. Tormohlen	4	38	2	10	.200	3	4	.750	18	6	7	0	7	1.2
J. Washington	4	6	2	4	.500	0	0	.000	3	0	2	0	4	1.0
J. Mullins	4	13	1	9	.112	0	2	.500	4	0	5	0	3	0.8

*—Number of games disqualified on personal fouls.

NBA SEASON STATISTICS

NEW INDIVIDUAL AND TEAM RECORDS

Most Players Scoring In Double Figures—7 by Balt., Tie, 1965-6
                          7 by Boston, Tie, 1965-6
Highest Field Goal Average—.540 by Wilt Chamberlain, Phil., 1965-6
                          .536 by John Green, Balt., 1965-6
Most Free Thows Made—840 by Jerry West, L.A., 1965-6
Most Consecutive Games Played—917 by John Kerr, Balt., 10/31/54 thru
    11/4/65
Most Consecutive Games, No Disqualifications (on Personals)—543 by Wilt
    Chamberlain, Phil., 10/24/59 thru 3 20 66
Most Seasons With Over 2,000 Points—7 by Wilt Chamberlain, Phil.
League Leader in Scoring—7 by Wilt Chamberlain, Phil.
All-Time League High Scorer—21,486 by Wilt Chamberlain, Phil.
Most Players Scoring 1,000 Points—6 by St. Louis 1965-6
Tying records compiled by Syracuse 1960-1 and Philadelphia 1964-5
Most Points Scored in One Game—W. Chamberlain, Phila., 65 vs. Los
    Angeles 2/7/66
Most Free Throws in One Game—R. Barry, San Francisco 21 @ N.Y., 12/14/65
Most Rebounds in One Game—W. Chamberlain, Phila., 42 vs. Boston 1/14/66
Most Assists in One Game—O. Robertson, Cinc., 22 vs. New York 3/5/66
Most Personal Fouls—Z. Beaty, St. Louis 344
Most Games Disqualified—T. Sanders, Boston 19

INDIVIDUAL SCORING LEADERS

	G	FG	FT	PTS	AVG.
W. Chamberlain, Phil.	79	1078	501	2649	33.5
J. West, LA	79	818	840	2476	31.4
O. Robertson, Cin.	76	818	742	2378	31.3
R. Barry, SF	80	745	569	2059	25.7
W. Bellamy, NY	80	695	430	1820	22.8
H. Greer, Phil.	80	703	413	1819	22.7
D. Barnett, NY	75	631	467	1729	23.1
J. Lucas, Cin.	79	690	313	1697	21.5
Z. Beaty, St. L.	80	616	424	1656	20.7
S. Jones, Bos.	68	626	325	1577	23.2
E. Miles, Det.	80	634	298	1566	19.6
D. Ohl, Balt.	73	593	316	1502	20.6
A. Smith, Cin.	80	531	408	1470	18.4
G. Rodgers, SF	79	586	296	1468	18.6
R. Scott, Det.	79	544	323	1411	17.9
B. Howell, Balt.	79	481	402	1364	17.3
K. Loughery, Balt.	74	526	297	1349	18.2
J. Havlicek, Bos.	71	530	274	1334	18.8
D. DeBusschere, Det.	79	525	249	1297	16.4
L. Wilkens, St. L.	69	411	422	1244	18.0

FIELD GOAL PERCENTAGE LEADERS

(Minimum 210 or more)

	FG	FGA	PCT.
W. Chamberlain, Phil.	1074	1990	.540
J. Green, Balt.	358	668	.536
W. Bellamy, NY	695	1373	.506
A. Attles, SF	364	724	.503
H. Hairston, Cin.	398	814	.489
B. Howell, Balt.	481	986	.488
B. Boozer, LA	365	754	.484
O. Robertson, Cin.	818	1723	.475
Z. Beaty, St. L.	616	1301	.473
J. West, LA	818	1731	.473

FREE THROW PERCENTAGE LEADERS

(Minimum 210)

	FT	FTA	PCT.
L. Siegfried, Bos.	274	311	.881
R. Barry, SF	569	660	.862
H. Komives, NY	241	280	.861
J. West, LA	840	977	.860
A. Smith, Cin.	408	480	.850
O. Robertson, Cin.	742	881	.842
P. Neumann, SF	265	317	.836
K. Loughery, Balt.	297	358	.830
R. Guerin, St. L.	362	466	.812
H. Greer, Phil.	413	514	.804

LEADERS IN ASSISTS

	G	NO.	AVG.
O. Robertson, Cin.	76	847	11.1
G. Rodgers, SF	79	846	10.7
K. C. Jones, Bos.	80	503	6.3
J. West, LA	79	480	6.1
H. Komives, NY	80	425	5.3
L. Wilkens, St. L.	69	429	6.2
W. Chamberlain, Phil.	79	414	5.2
W. Hazzard, LA	80	393	4.9
R. Guerin, St. L.	80	388	4.9
H. Greer, Phil.	80	384	4.8

LEADERS IN REBOUNDS

	G	NO.	AVG.
W. Chamberlain, Phil.	79	1943	24.6
B. Russell, Bos.	78	1779	22.8
J. Lucas, Cin.	79	1668	21.1
N. Thurmond, SF	73	1312	18.0
W. Bellamy, NY	80	1254	15.7
Z. Beaty, St. L.	80	1086	13.6
B. Bridges St. L.	78	951	12.2
D. DeBusschere, Det.	79	916	11.6
W. Reed, NY	76	883	11.6
R. Barry, SF	80	850	10.6

TEAM STATISTICS

	G	Field Goals			Free Throws			Rbnd	Miscellaneous			Scoring Average		
		Made	Att.	Pct.	Made	Att.	Pct.		Asst	PF	D*	For	Agst	Dif.
Boston	80	3488	8367	.417	2038	2758	.739	5591	1795	2012	39	112.7	107.8	4.9
Philadelphia	80	3650	8189	.446	2087	3141	.664	5652	1905	2094	39	117.3	112.7	4.6
Los Angeles	80	3597	8109	.444	2363	3057	.773	5334	1936	2035	25	119.5	116.4	3.1
Cincinnati	80	3610	8123	.444	2204	2906	.758	5559	1818	2033	24	117.8	116.6	1.2
St. Louis	80	3379	7836	.431	2155	2870	.751	5167	1782	2179	47	111.4	112.0	-0.6
Baltimore	80	3599	8210	.438	2267	3186	.712	5542	1890	2199	52	118.3	119.5	-1.2
New York	80	3559	7910	.450	2217	3078	.720	5119	1896	2227	48	116.7	119.3	-2.6
San Francisco	80	3557	8512	.418	2129	2879	.730	5727	1872	2069	37	115.5	118.2	-2.7
Detroit	80	3475	8502	.409	1877	2734	.687	5427	1569	2016	27	110.3	117.2	-6.9

INDIVIDUAL STATISTICS, TEAM BY TEAM

BALTIMORE

	G	Min-utes	FG Made	FG Att.	FG Pct.	Ft. Made	Ft. Att.	Ft. Pct.	Re-bnd	As-sist	PF	D*	Tot. Pts.	Avg.
D. Ohl	73	2645	593	1334	.445	316	430	.734	280	290	208	1	1502	20.6
B. Howell	79	2328	481	986	.488	402	551	.730	773	155	306	12	1364	17.3
K. Loughery	74	2455	526	1264	.416	297	358	.830	227	356	273	8	1349	18.2
J. Green***	79	1645	358	668	.536	202	388	.521	645	117	183	3	918	11.6
J. Green*	72	2191	315	589	.535	187	357	.524	571	96	162	10	817	11.3
J. Barnes***	73	1437	348	818	.425	212	310	.684	755	94	283	10	908	12.4
J. Barnes**	66	1928	308	728	.423	182	268	.679	683	85	250	10	798	12.1
J. Kerr	71	1770	286	692	.413	209	272	.768	586	225	148	1	781	11.0
J. Egan***	76	1644	259	574	.451	173	227	.762	183	273	167	3	691	9.1
J. Egan**	69	1586	254	558	.455	166	217	.765	181	259	163	9	674	9.8
G. Johnson	42	1284	273	661	.413	131	178	.736	546	114	136	1	677	16.1
B. Ferry	66	1229	188	457	.411	105	131	.802	215	25	134	2	481	7.3
J. Sloan	59	952	120	289	.415	98	139	.705	230	110	176	5	338	5.7
B. Warley***	57	773	116	284	.409	64	97	.660	217	25	129	2	296	5.2
B. Warley**	56	767	115	281	.409	64	97	.660	131	25	128	2	294	5.3
W. Hightower	24	460	63	186	.339	57	78	.731	102	35	61	0	183	7.6
W. Bellamy	8	268	56	124	.452	40	67	.597	100	18	32	0	152	19.0
W. Somerset	8	98	18	43	.419	9	11	.818	15	9	21	0	45	5.6
G. Bradds	3	15	2	6	.333	3	4	.750	8	1	1	0	7	2.3
T. McReynolds	5	28	1	12	.083	1	2	.500	6	1	0	0	3	0.6

*—Number of games disqualified on Personal Fouls

BOSTON

	G	Minutes	FG Made	FG Att.	FG Pct.	Ft. Made	Ft. Att.	Ft. Pct.	Rebnd	Assist	Per Fls.	D*	Tot. Pts.	Avg. Pts.
Sam Jones	68	2155	626	1335	.469	325	407	.799	347	216	170	0	1577	23.2
J. Havlicek	71	2175	530	1328	.399	274	349	.785	423	210	158	4	1334	18.8
L. Russell	78	3386	391	943	.415	223	405	.551	1779	371	221	1	1005	12.9
L. Siegfried	71	1675	349	825	.423	274	311	.881	196	165	157	1	972	13.7
T. Sanders	72	1896	349	816	.428	211	276	.764	508	90	317	19	909	12.6
D. Nelson	75	1765	271	618	.439	223	326	.684	403	79	187	1	765	10.2
W. Naulls	71	1433	328	815	.402	104	131	.794	319	72	197	4	760	10.7
K. C. Jones	80	2710	240	619	.388	209	303	.690	304	503	243	4	689	8.6
M. Counts	67	1021	221	549	.403	120	145	.826	432	50	207	5	562	8.4
R. Bonham	39	312	76	207	.367	52	61	.852	35	11	29	0	204	5.2
W. Sauldsberry	39	530	80	249	.321	11	22	.500	142	15	94	0	171	4.4
J. Thompson	10	72	14	30	.467	4	6	.667	30	3	15	0	32	3.2
S. Green	10	92	12	31	.387	8	16	.500	11	9	16	0	32	3.2
R. Watts	1	3	1	2	.500	0	0	.000	1	1	1	0	2	2.0

PHILADELPHIA

	G	Minutes	FG Made	FG Att.	FG Pct.	Ft. Made	Ft. Att.	Ft. Pct.	Rebnd	Assist	Per Fls.	D*	Tot. Pts.	Avg. Pts.
W. Chamberlain	79	3737	1074	1990	.540	501	976	.513	1943	414	171	0	2649	33.5
H. Greer	80	3326	703	1580	.445	413	514	.804	473	384	315	6	1819	22.7
C. Walker	80	2603	443	982	.451	335	468	.716	636	201	238	3	1221	15.3
B. Cunningham	80	2134	431	1011	.426	281	443	.634	599	207	301	12	1143	14.3
L. Jones	80	2196	296	799	.370	128	172	.744	169	273	250	6	720	9.0
L. Jackson	79	1966	246	614	.401	158	214	.738	676	132	216	2	650	8.2
D. Gambee	72	1068	168	437	.384	159	187	.850	273	71	189	3	495	6.9
A. Bianchi	78	1312	214	560	.382	66	98	.673	134	134	232	4	494	6.3
J. Ward	66	838	67	189	.354	39	60	.650	89	80	163	3	173	2.6
A. Heyman***	17	120	18	52	.346	14	22	.636	17	11	23	0	50	2.9
A. Heyman**	6	20	3	9	.333	4	5	.800	7	4	4	0	10	1.7
J. Weiss	7	30	3	9	.333	0	0	.000	4	4	10	0	6	0.9
J. Branson	5	14	1	6	.167	3	4	.750	7	1	4	0	5	1.0
B. Warley	1	6	1	3	.333	0	0	.000	2	0	1	0	2	2.0

CINCINNATI

	G	Min-utes	FG Made	FG Att.	FG Pct.	Ft. Made	Ft. Att.	Ft. Pct.	Re-bnd	As-sist	Per Fls.	D*	Tot. Pts.	Avg. Pts.
O. Robertson	76	3493	818	1723	.475	742	881	.842	586	847	227	1	2378	31.3
J. Lucas	79	3517	690	1523	.453	317	403	.787	1668	213	274	5	1697	21.5
A. Smith	80	2982	531	1310	.405	408	480	.850	287	256	276	11	1470	18.4
H. Hairston	72	1794	398	814	.489	220	321	.685	546	44	216	3	1016	14.1
W. Hawkins	79	2126	273	605	.452	116	209	.555	525	99	216	4	662	8.4
W. Embry	80	1882	232	564	.411	141	234	.603	575	81	287	9	605	7.6
J. Twyman	73	943	224	498	.450	95	117	.812	168	60	122	1	543	7.4
J. McGlocklin	72	852	153	363	.421	67	79	.785	133	88	77	0	368	5.1
C. Dierking	57	782	134	322	.416	50	82	.610	245	43	113	0	318	5.6
T. Thacker	50	478	84	207	.406	15	38	.395	119	61	85	0	183	3.7
G. Wilson	47	276	54	138	.391	27	42	.643	98	17	56	0	135	2.9
A. Heyman	11	100	15	43	.349	10	17	.588	13	7	19	0	40	3.6
B. Olsen	4	36	3	8	.375	1	3	.333	13	2	4	0	7	1.8
J. Arnette	3	14	1	6	.167	0	0	.000	0	0	3	0	2	0.7

*—Number of games disqualified on personal fouls.
**—Team Total
***—Combined Player Total

ST. LOUIS

	G	Min-utes	FG Made	FG Att.	FG Pct.	Ft. Made	Ft. Att.	Ft. Pct.	Re-bnd	As-sist	Per Fls.	D*	Tot. Pts.	Avg. Pts.
Z. Beaty	80	3072	616	1301	.473	424	559	.758	1086	125	344	15	1656	20.7
L. Wilkens	69	2692	411	954	.431	422	532	.793	322	429	248	4	1244	18.0
R. Guerin	80	2363	414	998	.415	362	446	.812	314	388	256	7	1190	14.9
C. Hagan	74	1851	419	942	.445	176	206	.854	234	164	177	11	1014	13.7
B. Bridges	78	2677	377	927	.407	257	364	.706	951	208	333	3	1011	13.0
J. Caldwell***	79	1857	268	600	.438	179	254	.705	436	126	203	1	1001	12.7
J. Caldwell**	46	1141	306	728	.447	168	236	.717	246	61	140	3	655	14.2
R. Thorn***	73	1739	163	385	.423	78	113	.690	210	145	144	0	780	10.7
R. Thorn**	46	924	158	393	.402	68	120	.567	109	81	77	0	404	8.8
J. Washington	65	1104	144	324	.444	54	82	.659	353	60	176	4	384	5.9
J. Tormohlen	71	775	104	243	.428	54	86	.628	314	43	138	3	342	4.8
J. Barnhill	31	691	113	296	.382	29	36	.806	91	83	58	0	255	8.5
J. Mullins	44	587	72	192	.375	46	62	.742	69	66	68	1	190	5.8
C. Vaughn	19	445	70	173	.405	35	61	.574	46	36	39	0	175	10.0
P. Silas	46	586	37	78	.474	101	120	.844	236	22	72	0	175	3.8
J. Tresvant	15	213	35	73	.479	27	32	.844	85	10	43	0	101	6.7
M. Farmer	9	79	13	30	.433	4	5	.800	18	6	10	0	30	3.3

SAN FRANCISCO

	G	Minutes	FG Made	FG Att.	FG Pct.	Ft. Made	Ft. Att.	Ft. Pct.	Re-bnd	As-sist	Per Fls.	D*	Tot. Pts.	Avg. Pts.
R. Barry	80	2990	745	1698	.439	569	660	.862	850	173	297	2	2059	25.7
G. Rodgers	79	2902	586	1571	.373	296	407	.727	421	846	241	6	1468	18.6
N. Thurmond	73	2891	454	1119	.406	280	428	.654	1312	111	223	7	1188	16.3
T. Meschery	80	2383	401	895	.448	224	293	.765	716	81	285	7	1026	12.8
P. Neumann	66	1729	343	817	.420	265	317	.836	208	184	174	5	951	14.4
A. Attles	79	2053	364	724	.503	154	252	.611	322	225	265	4	882	11.2
M. McLemore	80	1467	225	528	.426	142	191	.743	488	55	197	0	592	7.4
F. Hetzel	56	722	160	401	.399	63	92	.685	290	27	121	2	383	6.8
G. Phillips	67	867	106	303	.350	54	87	.621	134	113	97	1	266	4.0
K. Erickson	65	646	95	267	.356	43	65	.662	162	38	91	1	233	3.6
B. Olsen**	59	602	81	193	.420	39	88	.443	192	20	81	1	201	3.4
B. Olsen***	57	566	78	185	.422	38	85	.447	175	18	77	1	194	3.4
W. Frazier	2	9	0	4	.000	1	2	.500			1	0	1	0.5

*.—Number of games disqualified on personal fouls.
**.—Team Total
***.—Combined Player Total

LOS ANGELES

	G	Minutes	FG Made	FG Att.	FG Pct.	Ft. Made	Ft. Att.	Ft. Pct.	Re-bnd	As-sist	Per Fls.	D*	Tot. Pts.	Avg. Pts.
J. West	79	3218	818	1731	.473	840	977	.860	562	480	243	1	2476	31.4
R. LaRusso	77	2316	410	897	.457	350	445	.787	660	165	261	9	1170	15.2
W. Hazzard	80	2198	458	1003	.457	182	257	.708	219	393	224	0	1098	13.7
E. Baylor	65	1975	415	1034	.401	249	337	.738	621	224	157	0	1079	16.6
L. Ellis	80	2219	393	927	.424	186	256	.727	735	74	232	3	972	12.2
B. Boozer	78	1847	365	754	.484	223	289	.772	548	87	196	1	955	12.2
J. King	76	1499	238	545	.437	94	115	.817	204	223	181	0	570	7.5
G. Goodrich	65	1008	203	503	.404	103	149	.691	130	103	103	1	509	7.8
D. Imhoff	77	1413	151	337	.448	77	136	.566	509	113	234	7	379	4.9
G. Wiley	67	1386	123	289	.426	43	76	.566	490	63	171	3	289	4.3

NEW YORK

	G	Min-utes	FG Made	FG Att.	FG Pct.	Ft. Made	Ft. Att.	Ft. Pct.	Re-bnd	As-sist	Per Fls.	D*	Tot. Pts.	Avg. Pts.
W. Bellamy***	80	3352	695	1373	.506	430	689	.624	1254	235	294	9	1820	22.8
W. Bellamy**	72	3084	639	1249	.512	390	622	.627	1152	217	262	7	1668	23.2
D. Barnett	75	2589	631	1344	.469	467	605	.772	310	259	235	6	1729	23.1
W. Reed	76	2589	438	1009	.434	302	399	.757	883	91	323	13	1178	15.5
H. Komives	80	2612	436	1116	.391	241	280	.861	281	425	278	5	1113	13.9
D. Stallworth	80	1893	373	820	.455	258	376	.686	492	186	237	11	1004	12.6
D. Van Arsdale	79	2289	359	838	.428	251	351	.715	376	184	235	4	969	12.3
E. Bryant	71	1193	212	449	.472	74	101	.733	170	216	215	5	498	7.0
B. Clemens	70	877	161	391	.412	54	78	.692	183	67	113	0	376	5.4
T. Gola	74	1127	100	271	.450	82	105	.781	289	191	207	3	326	4.4
L. Chappell	46	545	100	238	.420	46	78	.590	127	26	64	1	246	5.3
J. Barnes	7	263	40	90	.444	30	42	.714	72	9	33	0	110	15.7
J. Green	7	208	43	79	.544	15	31	.484	74	11	21	0	101	14.4
J. Egan	7	58	5	16	.313	7	10	.700	2	14	4	0	17	2.4

*—Number of games disqualified on personal fouls.
**—Team Total
***—Combined Player Total

DETROIT

	G	Min-utes	FG Made	FG Att.	FG Pct.	Ft. Made	Ft. Att.	Ft. Pct.	Re-bnd	As-sist	Per Fls.	D*	Tot. Pts.	Avg. Pts.
E. Miles	80	2788	634	1418	.447	298	402	.741	302	221	203	2	1566	19.6
R. Scott	79	2652	544	1309	.416	323	435	.743	755	238	209	1	1411	17.9
D. DeBusschere	79	2696	524	1284	.408	249	378	.659	916	209	252	5	1297	16.4
T. VanArsdale	79	2041	312	834	.374	209	290	.721	309	205	251	1	833	10.5
T. Strawder	79	2180	250	613	.408	176	256	.688	820	78	305	10	676	8.6
J. Barnhill***	76	1617	243	600	.401	113	184	.614	203	196	134	0	599	7.9
J. Barnhill**	45	926	139	363	.383	59	98	.602	112	113	76	2	337	7.5
J. Tresvant***	61	969	171	400	.428	142	190	.747	364	72	179	2	484	7.9
J. Tresvant**	46	756	134	322	.416	115	158	.728	728	62	136	1	383	8.3
C. Vaughn***	56	1219	182	474	.384	106	144	.726	109	140	99	0	470	8.4
C. Vaughn**	37	774	110	282	.390	60	82	.732	63	104	60	1	280	7.6
R. Kojis	60	783	182	439	.415	76	141	.539	260	42	94	0	440	7.3
R. Reed	57	997	186	524	.355	54	100	.540	339	92	133	1	426	7.5
R. Thorn	27	815	143	343	.417	90	123	.732	101	64	67	0	376	13.9
J. Caldwell	33	716	143	338	.423	60	88	.682	190	65	63	4	346	10.5
B. Buntin	42	713	118	299	.395	88	143	.615	252	36	119	0	324	7.7
D. Butcher	15	285	45	96	.469	18	34	.529	33	30	40	4	108	7.2
B. Warlick	10	78	11	38	.289	2	6	.333	16	10	8	0	24	2.4

*—Number of games disqualified on personal fouls.
**—Team Total
***—Combined Player Total

NATIONAL BASKETBALL ASSOCIATION
COLLEGE DRAFT 1966

DETROIT
Dave Bing
  Syracuse
Dorrie Murrey
  Detroit
Oliver Darden
  Michigan
Jeff Congdon
  Brigham Young
William Pickens
  Georgia Southern
Carroll Hooser
  So. Methodist
Ted Manning
  No. Carolina Col.
George McNeil
  So. Illinois

NEW YORK
Cazzie Russell
  Michigan
Henry Aiken
  Morehead
Stewart Johnson
  Murray State
Lee DeFore
  Auburn
Ron Jackson
  Clark (Atlanta)
George Fisher
  Utah
Mike Dabich
  New Mexico St.
Mike Silliman
  Army

SAN FRANCISCO
Clyde Lee
  Vanderbilt
Joe Ellis
  San Francisco
Steve Chubin
  Rhode Island
Steve Vacendak
  Duke
Tom Kerwin
  Centenary
Jim Pitts
  Northwestern
Lon Hughey
  Fresno State
Ken Washington
  U.C.L.A.

ST. LOUIS
Lou Hudson
  Minnesota
Dick Snyder
  Davidson
Tommy Kron
  Kentucky
Bob McIntyre
  St. John's
Dick Nemelka
  Brigham Young
Lonnie Wright
  Colorado St.
Ray Neary
  Wilmington (NC)
Brian Williams
  Xavier, Ohio

BALTIMORE
Jack Marin
  Duke
Neil Johnson
  Creighton
Dave Wagnon
  Idaho St.
George Peeples
  Iowa
John Beasley (from Bos.)
  Texas A & M
John Jones
  L.A. State
Jeff Neuman
  Pennsylvania
Dave Mills
  DePaul
Roland West
  Cincinnati

CINCINNATI
Walt Wesley
  Kansas
Jerry Lee Wells
  Okla. City
James Ware
  Okla. City
Charles Schmaus
  V.M.I.
Rick Parks
  St. Louis
Steve Cunningham
  Western Kentucky
Gary Schull
  Florida State
Ron Krick
  Cincinnati

LOS ANGELES
Jerry Chambers
  Utah
Henry Finkel (from
  Chicago)
  Dayton
John Block
  U.S.C.
Archie Clark
  Minnesota
Stan Washington
  Michigan St.
Keith Thomas
  Vanderbilt
Tab Jackson
  Idaho College
John Wetzel
  V.P.I.

BOSTON
Jim Barnett
  Oregon
Leon Clark
  Wyoming
Gary Turner
  T.C.U.
(To Baltimore)
John Austin
  Boston Col.
Charlie Hunter
  Okla. City
Jerry Ward
  Maryland
Russ Gumina
  San Francisco

PHILADELPHIA
Matt Guokas
  St. Joseph's
Bill Melchionni
  Villanova
Don Freeman
  Illinois
Ken Wilburn
  Central St. (Ohio)
Tom Duff
  St. Joseph's
Austin "Red" Robbins
  Univ. of Tennessee
  PASS
  PASS

NATIONAL BASKETBALL ASSOCIATION
COLLEGE DRAFT 1966 (Cont'd)

CHICAGO
Dave Schellhase
  Purdue
(To Los Angeles)
Irwin Mueller
  San Francisco
Eddie Bodkin
  Eastern Kentucky
Jim Williams
  Temple
Larry Humes
  Evansville
John Coneaux
  Grambling
Stan Curtis
  Michigan State
Gene Summers
  No. Michigan

THE NBA ALL-STAR GAME

WEST

	G-ST	F-FT	R	A	PF	P
Barry	4-10	2- 4	2	2	6	10
Beaty	0-11	10-13	18	2	2	10
DeBusschere	1-14	2- 2	6	1	1	4
Howell	3-11	1- 2	2	2	4	7
LaRusso	4-10	3- 7	3	2	2	11
Miles	8-16	1- 5	1	0	1	17
Ohl	7-16	2- 3	4	2	2	16
Rodgers	4-11	0- 0	7	11	4	8
Thurmond	3-16	1- 3	16	1	1	7
West	1- 5	2- 2	1	0	2	4
Totals	35-120	24-41	60	22	25	94

EAST

	G-ST	F-FT	R	A	PF	P
Chamberlain	8-11	5- 9	9	3	2	21
Greer	4-13	1- 1	5	1	4	9
Havlicek	6-16	6- 6	6	1	2	18
Jones	5-12	2- 2	2	5	0	12
Lucas	4-11	2- 2	19	0	2	10
Reed	7-11	2- 2	8	1	3	16
Robertson	6-12	5- 6	10	8	0	17
Russell	1- 4	0- 0	10	2	2	2
Smith	9-18	6- 6	8	3	5	24
Walker	3-10	2- 3	6	4	2	8
Totals	53-118	31-37	83	28	22	137
WEST	18	18	32		26—	94
EAST	33	30	38		36—137	

Team Fouls—East 22, West 25.
Fouled Out—Barry.
Referees—Norm Drucker and John Vanek.
Attendance—13,653.

NCAA CHAMPIONSHIP

TEXAS WESTERN (72)

	G	F	P
Hill	7	6-9	20
Artis	5	5-5	15
Shed	1	1-1	3
Lattin	5	6-6	16
Worsley	2	4-6	8
Flourney	1	0-0	2
Cager	1	6-7	8
Totals	22	28-34	72

KENTUCKY (65)

	G	F	P
Dampier	7	5-5	19
Kron	3	0-0	6
Conley	4	2-2	10
Riley	8	3-4	19
Jaracz	3	1-2	7
Berger	2	0-0	4
Totals	27	11-13	65

Half-time score—Texas Western 34, Kentucky 31.
Fouled out—Conley, Jaracz.
Attendance—14,253.

NCAA CONSOLATION GAME

DUKE (79)

	G	F	P
Verga	7	1-1	15
Riedy	2	0-0	4
Marin	9	5-5	23
Vacendak	5	1-4	11
Lewis	5	4-5	14
Wendelin	2	0-2	4
Kennedy	0	0-0	0
Barone	1	0-0	2
Chapman	2	0-1	4
Kolodziej	1	0-0	2
Liccardo	0	0-2	0
Totals	34	11-20	79

UTAH (77)

	G	F	P
Tate	1	2-5	4
Jackson	6	2-2	14
MacKay	4	5-6	13
Ockel	5	0-0	10
Chambers	11	10-12	32
Black	2	0-1	4
Day	0	0-0	0
Totals	29	19-26	77

Halftime score—Duke 41, Utah 37.
Fouled out—Riedy.

NCAA SEMI-FINALS

KENTUCKY (83)

	G	F	P
Conley	3	4-4	10
Riley	8	3-4	19
Jaracz	3	2-3	8
Dampier	11	1-2	23
Kron	5	2-2	12
Tallent	1	2-2	4
Berger	1	5-6	7
Gamble	0	0-1	0
Totals	32	19-24	83

DUKE (79)

	G	F	P
Marin	11	7-10	29
Riedy	2	2-2	6
Lewis	9	3-3	21
Verga	2	0-0	4
Vacendak	7	3-3	17
Wendelin	1	0-1	2
Liccardo	0	0-0	0
Barone	0	0-0	0
Totals	32	15-19	79

Half-time score—Duke 42, Kentucky 41.
Fouled out—Riley, Jaracz, Vacendak.

TEXAS WESTERN (85)

	G	F	P
Hill	5	8-10	18
Artis	10	2-3	22
Shed	2	5-6	9
Lattin	5	1-1	11
Flourney	3	2-2	8
Cager	2	1-1	5
Wersley	5	2-3	12
Armstrong	0	0-1	0
Totals	32	21-27	85

UTAH (78)

	G	F	P
Tate	0	1-3	1
Jackson	3	2-2	8
Mackay	4	6-9	14
Ockel	1	3-3	5
Chambers	14	10-12	38
Black	3	2-4	8
Lake	1	0-0	2
Day	1	0-0	2
Totals	27	24-33	78

Half-time score—Texas Western 42, Utah 39.
Fouled out—Lattin, Flourney, Tate.

NIT CHAMPIONSHIP

BRIGHAM YOUNG (97)

	G	F	P
Kramer	9	2	20
James	0	0	0
Hill	9	3	21
Ruffner	1	0	2
Raymond	10	1	21
Fisher	0	0	0
Gongdon	5	1	11
Schouten	1	0	2
Nemelka	5	5	15
Jimas	2	1	5
Eakins	0	0	0
Totals	42	13	97

NYU (84)

	G	F	P
McKenzie	10	7	27
Kaplan	9	0	18
Silen	3	3	9
Graham	8	2	18
Dyer	5	2	12
Totals	35	14	84

NIT CONSOLATION GAME

VILLANOVA (76)

	G	F	P
Schaffer	6	2	14
Crews	7	1	15
Stinger	0	0	0
Gaidjunas	1	0	2
McGuire	1	0	2
Livers	0	0	0
Coleman	4	0	8
Trainor	0	2	2
Krines	1	2	4
Melchionni	13	3	29
Totals	33	10	76

ARMY (65)

	G	F	P
Helkie	4	1	9
Schrage	0	2	2
Schutsky	7	5	19
Noonan	5	7	17
Murray	3	5	11
Seigle	0	1	1
Hughes	1	2	2
Jordan	2	0	4
Mikula	0	0	0
Totals	22	21	65

THE COLLEGE ALL-STAR GAME

EAST (126)

	G	F	P
Conley	3	0-0	6
Bing	4	3-4	11
Finkel	4	5-7	13
Vacendak	6	0-0	12
Schellhase	7	3-3	17
Kron	4	0-0	8
Russell	8	8-9	24
Snyder	1	1-2	3
Melchionni	8	0-0	16
McIntyre	7	2-2	16
Totals	52	22-27	126

WEST (99)

	G	F	P
Chambers	9	1-1	19
Block	1	3-3	5
Wesley	5	0-0	10
Namelka	4	3-3	11
Barnett	8	3-4	19
Beasley	2	1-2	5
Ellis	4	0-2	8
Wright	8	0-1	16
Malaise	2	0-1	4
Hooser	1	0-1	2
Totals	44	11-28	99

Half-time score—East 56, West 45.
Attendance—8,000.

THE ALL-AMERICA PLAYERS

THE AP SELECTIONS

FIRST TEAM

Cazzie Russell, Michigan, 6-foot-5 senior, hometown, Chicago.
Clyde Lee, Vanderbilt, 6-9 senior, Nashville.
Dave Schallhase, Purdue, 6-4 senior, Indianapolis
Dave Bing, Syracuse, 6-3 senior, Washington, D.C.
Louis Dampier, Kentucky, 6-0 junior, Indianapolis.

SECOND TEAM

Jim Walker, Providence, 6-3 junior, Boston.
Jack Marin, Duke, 6-6 senior, Farrell, Pa.
Bob Verga, Duke, 6-0 junior, Sea Girt, N.J.
Dick Snyder, Davidson, 6-5 senior, North Canton, Ohio.
Matt Guokas, Jr., St. Joseph's, 6-5 junior, Philadelphia.

THIRD TEAM

Walt Wesley, Kansas, 6-11 senior, Fort Myers, Fla.
Henry Finkel, Dayton, 6-11 senior, Union City, N.J.
Bob Lewis, North Carolina, 6-3 junior, Washington, D.C.
Thad Jaracz, Kentucky, 6-5 sophomore, Lexington, Ky.
Pat Riley, Kentucky, 6-3 junior, Schenectady, N.Y.

THE UPI SELECTIONS

FIRST TEAM—Cazzie Russell, Michigan; Dave Schellhase, Purdue; Clyde Lee, Vanderbilt; Dave Bing, Syracuse; Jim Walker, Providence.
SECOND TEAM—Louis Dampier, Kentucky; Walt Wesley, Kansas; Bob Verga, Duke; Matt Guokas, St. Joseph's; Dick Snyder, Davidson.
THIRD TEAM—Pat Riley, Kentucky; Jack Marin, Duke; Henry Finkel, Dayton; Louis Hudson, Minnesota; John Austin, Boston College.

THE NEA SELECTIONS

FIRST TEAM

Pos.	Name	School	Cl.	Hgt.	Wgt.	Hometown
F—Dave Schellhase		Purdue	Sr.	6-4	205	Evansville, Ind.
F—Clyde Lee		Vanderbilt	Sr.	6-9	215	Nashville, Tenn.
C—Walt Wesley		Kansas	Sr.	6-11	225	Ft. Myers, Fla.
G—Cazzie Russell		Michigan	Sr.	6-6	218	Chicago, Ill.
G—Dave Bing		Syracuse	Sr.	6-3	185	Washington, D.C.

SECOND TEAM

Pos.	Name	School	Cl.	Hgt.	Wgt.	Hometown
F—Dick Snyder		Davidson	Sr.	6-5	210	N. Canton, Ohio
F—Lou Hudson		Minnesota	Sr.	6-5	207	Greensboro, N.C.
C—Henry Finkel		Dayton	Sr.	6-11	240	Union City, N.J.
G—Matt Guokas		St. Joe. (Pa.)	Jr.	6-5	185	Philadelphia
G—Jim Walker		Providence	Jr.	6-3	200	Boston

HONORABLE MENTION—Bob Verga, Duke; Mike Silliman, Army; John Austin, Boston College; Edgar Lacey, UCLA; Pat Riley, Kentucky; Clem Haskins, Western Kentucky; Jack Marin, Duke; Oliver Darden, Michigan; Elvin Hayes, Houston; Joe Ellis, San Francisco; Westley Unseld, Louisville; John Beasley, Texas A&M; Rich Parks, St. Louis; Larry Humes, Evansville; Don May, Dayton; Dick Nemelka, Brigham Young.

N.A.I.A. ALL-AMERICA TEAMS
Selected by the Coaches

FIRST TEAM

		POS.	HT.	YEAR
Curt Gammell	Pacific Lutheran (Wash.)	F	6-7	Senior
Jim Shuler	Carson-Newman (Tenn.)	F	6-6	Senior
Earl Beechum	Midwestern (Texas)	F	6-5	Junior
Al Tucker	Oklahoma Baptist	F	6-8	Junior
Ken Wilburn	Central State (Ohio)	C	6-6	Senior
Pat Caldwell	Rockhurst (Mo.)	C	6-6	Senior
Gene Summers	Northern Michigan	G	6-0	Soph.
Henry Logan	Western Carolina (N.C.)	G	6-2	Junior
Jimmy Rose	Georgia Southern	G	5-11	Senior
Gary Liberatore	New Haven (Conn.)			

SECOND TEAM

Al Albers	Upper Iowa	F	6-5	Senior
Johnny Comeaux	Grambling (La.)	F	6-6	Senior
Marlbert Pradd	Dillard (La.)	F	6-2	Junior
Jim Chroust	Pittsburg State (Kan.)	C	6-7	Senior
Isidore Schmeising	St. Cloud State (Minn.)	C	6-8	Senior
Richard Pitts	Norfolk State (Va.)	C	6-6	Senior
Earl Monroe	Winston-Salem State (N.C.)	G	6-2	Junior
Don Hakala	Linfield (Ore.)	G	6-0	Senior
Ron Jackson	Clark (Ga.)	G	5-11	Senior
Dewey Kalmer	Quincy (Ill.)	G	6-1	Senior

THIRD TEAM

Richard Harris	Manchester (Ind.)	F	6-5	Soph.
Roger Raspen	Millersville State (Pa.)	F	6-4	Junior
Darryl Meachem	Edinboro State (Pa.)	F	6-4	Junior
Russell Noll	McMurry (Texas)	F	6-4	Senior
Taft Jackson	College of Idaho	C	6-7	Senior
Zoilo Dominquez	Albuquerque (N. M.)	C	6-9	Junior
Gene Littles	High Point (N. C.)	G	6-1	Fresh.
Bobby Ritch	Valdosta State (Ga.)	G	6-1	Senior
Darryl Jones	St. Benedict's (Kan.)	G	6-5	Soph.
Bob Guy	Lakeland (Wis.)	G	5-11	Junior

NCAA SCORING LEADERS

	Games	Pts.	Avg.
1. Schellhase, Purdue _____	24	781	32.54
2. Wagnon, Idaho St. _____	26	845	32.50
3. Russell, Michigan _____	26	800	30.8
4. Chambers, Utah _____	31	892	28.8
5. Bing, Syracuse _____	28	794	28.4
6. Kerwin, Centenary _____	26	726	27.9
7. Freeman, Illinois _____	24	668	27.8
7. Beasley, Texas A&M _____	24	668	27.8
9. Melchionni, Villanova _____	29	801	27.6
10. Lewis, No. Carolina _____	27	740	27.4
11. Hayes, Houston _____	29	789	27.2
12. Wells, Okla. City _____	29	786	27.1
13. Marshall, LaSalle _____	25	674	27.0
14. Snyder, Davidson _____	28	753	26.9
15. Lloyd, Rutgers _____	24	635	26.5

THE HIGH-SCHOOL ALL-AMERICAS
Selected by *Scholastic Coach Magazine*

Name and School	Ht.	Ave.	Coach
Chuck Bavis (Garrett) Ind.	7-0	28.0	Ward Smith
Bob Lienhard (Rice) New York, N. Y.	6-11	25.0	Mike Browne
Dan Issel (Batavia) Ill.	6-9	25.0	Don Vandersnick
Gary Freeman (Borah) Boise, Idaho	6-9	21.3	Terry Conley
Dennis Awtrey (Blackford) San Jose, Cal.	6-9	28.8	Pat Dougherty
Mike Mardy (Memorial) West New York, N.J.	6-8½	28.8	Tony Bocchieri
Greg Douglas (Keokuk) Iowa	6-8	25.2	Bill Jones
John Hummer (Wash.-Lee) Arlington, Va.	6-7	15.0	Morris Levin
Elvin Ivory (C. W. Hayes) Birmingham, Ala.	6-7	31.0	Bill Scoggins
Rudy Tomjanovich (Hamtramck) Mich.	6-7	25.1	John Radwanski
Sam Robinson (Jefferson) Los Angeles, Cal.	6-7	24.7	Larry Hanson
Ken Durrett (Schenley) Pittsburgh, Pa.	6-6	27.5	Willard Fisher
Dave Sorenson (Findlay) Ohio	6-6	25.4	John Stozich
Doug Cook (Ridgewood) N. J.	6-6	23.4	Jim Bruni
Jim McMillan (Jefferson) Brooklyn, N. Y.	6-5	29.7	Sam Beckman
Perry Wallace (Pearl) Nashville, Tenn.	6-5	13.4	Cornelius Ridley
Doug Jackson (West) Shawnee Mission, Kan.	6-5	24.6	Clayton Henry
Ralph Ogden (Lincoln) San Jose, Cal.	6-5	24.2	Jack Richards
Mike Casey (Shelby Co.) Shelbyville, Ky.	6-4½	28.5	Bill Harrell
Jeff Petrie (Springfield) Delaware Co., Pa.	6-4	20.0	Harry Bell
Charlie Scott (Laurinberg Institute) N. C.	6-4	27.0	J. F. McDuffie
Rick Tannenberger (Little Rock Central) Ark.	6-4	20.3	Jim Cathcart
Fablen Mang (Jesuit) New Orleans, La.	6-4	26.3	Dick Francis
Jerry Kroll (Memorial) Spring Branch, Texas	6-4	24.0	Don Coleman
Chuck Moore (Polytechnic) Long Beach, Cal.	6-4	20.6	Will Foerster
Ron White (Boys Town) Neb.	6-3½	19.0	George Pfelfer
Bob Duklet (Livingston) N. J.	6-3½	32.7	Jack Waddon
Marshall Lewis (Technical) Boston, Mass.	6-3	31.7	Ed Grant
Roosevelt Philps (Troy) N. Y.	6-3	22.5	Jerry Pucci
Rick Mount (Lebanon) Ind.	6-3	33.0	Jim Rosenstihl
Rich Bradshaw (Marshall) Chicago, Ill.	6-3	20.0	Harv Hartenstein
Bob Hummell (Moundsville) W. Va.	6-2	36.3	Joe Pelaez
Jerry Francis (West) Columbus, Ohio	6-2	26.1	Fred Heischman
Frank Price (River Rouge) Mich.	6-1	18.0	Lofton Greene
Tom Little (Mackin) Washington, D. C.	6-0	25.5	Paul Furlong
Dean Meminger (Rice) New York, N. Y.	6-0	18.0	Mike Browne
Trent Gaines (Polytechnic) Long Beach, Cal.	6-0	19.6	Will Foerster
Don Crosby (Cony) Augusta, Maine	5-11	19.5	Dick Hunt
Calvin Murphy (Norwalk) Conn.	5-10	40.3	Jack Cronin
Billy Nickleberry (Jefferson) Portland, Ore.	5-8	26.9	Jack Riley